The first sales transaction

of the Jordan Marsh Company

was the sale of one yard of cherry colored ribbon

by Eben Jordan, its founder, to Louisa Bareiss, his friend.

Friendship is the basis of confidence,

and confidence is the basis of success.

# TALES OF
# THE OBSERVER

# Tales

## *of* The

# Observer

*by*

RICHARD H. EDWARDS, JR.

PUBLISHED BY JORDAN MARSH COMPANY
BOSTON, MASS.

TALES OF THE OBSERVER

*Copyright, 1950, by Richard H. Edwards, Jr.*

MANUFACTURED BY THE COLONIAL PRESS INC., CLINTON, MASS.

A COMPLETE NEW ENGLAND PRODUCT

These Tales are dedicated to the thousands of people of the yesterdays and today, both from within and without, through whose mutual and loyal efforts this great institution has reached its place of honored eminence.

*Richard A. Edwards jr.*

# CONTENTS

## Appendix

# TALES OF
# THE OBSERVER

## CHAPTER I

# MY EARLY YEARS

BACK in the days when Eben Dyer Jordan hadn't the price of a pipe in his pocket, he used to say to me, "Steady now, friend —there's a time for looking backward and a time for looking forward. This is the time for looking forward."

Eben usually knew what he was talking about. He may have been young, but he had a streak of common sense and stability as rugged as the coast of Maine and as keen as a Yankee fisherman's knife. Having thus spoken, he then looked forward so long and so far and with such sagacity that—thanks to him and his like —here I am at the Century Mark.

Yes, here I am 100 years of age, a centenarian in this Year of Our Lord 1951, and for the moment at least, it's a time for looking backward.

That's a centenarian's privilege, I believe—to look backward and to reminisce and to ramble among his thoughts and memories. And that's what they call me, The Observer—a quaint old man with a host of good stories to tell.

Just between ourselves, I don't feel half as old as the calendar

1

says I am. I suppose that's what comes of being the spirit of an organization like the Jordan Marsh Company. Jordan's is always moving a couple of turns ahead of the times, like a dolphin swerving ahead of a square-rigger —and that's what keeps me young in mind and heart and body, no matter how many winters fall behind me.

You'll have to admit I don't look old in the face. You've seen me many a time, gazing down at the framework of new Jordan construction—looking at you from the roadsides of Massachusetts highways—sometimes doing a short turn in the Jordan's advertisements in your daily newspapers.

In case you can't remember, I'm the New Englander who's pictured in the old tri-cornered hat—the one with the whimsical smile on his face and the long clay pipe in his hands.

Just between you and me, I think I'd get a much better smoke if they'd let me trade that old pipe of mine for one of the new briars in the Jordan Store for Men. Sometimes I get a wistful longing to shed my three-cornered top piece, too, and try one of the smart snap brims that other men buy in Jordan's, but my fellow-workers won't let me do that. They say I have to stay in character—the spirit of Jordan Marsh—something vital and typical of old New England's strength of honesty and vision and individuality.

"You're The Observer," they say to me. "We like you the way you are. You stay that way now, and tell us the tales of Jordan Marsh. Tell them so all the people of Boston and New England

2

will know the story and will be as pleased and as proud as we are."

They're right, of course; that's why I'm here. So I'll tell my tales the best I know how—the bits of light and shadow, of romance and adventure, of heart-tug and humor—all the elements that have helped to shape the character of Jordan Marsh in the past 100 years.

I remember it was back in the days of the Clipper Ships when I first came to know Eben Jordan. It was the Golden Age of New England sails. The spars and rigging of gallant vessels made a crazy network along the Boston waterfront, and the bowsprits of other New England craft were poking into faraway ports from Liverpool to the Java Straits.

Eben Jordan had been in Boston about 15 years before I got to meet him. He had come down from his home in Danville, Maine, in 1836—a 14-year-old youngster who had saved a stake of $2.75 by working from sunup to sundown on a hard-rock farm.

What with one thing and another, he had only $1.25 of his fortune left when he stepped from the Portland packet onto Boston soil and looked around to see where he could earn a piece of bread.

His ears picked up the news that there was room for a hired hand on a small farm in Roxbury. He walked to the farm and talked himself into the job, at $4 a month.

Eben stayed there two years, hoeing corn and potatoes, shearing the sheep and milking the cows. Then he left to go to work as an errand boy in a dry goods store owned by William P. Tenney and Company.

He never talked to me much about his first years in the retail business. Still, he must have shown real talent in the trade of that day for by the time he was 19 a merchant named Joshua Stetson had spotted the young man and had decided Eben was worth a

financial risk. He agreed to finance young Jordan in a store of his own at 168 Hanover Street.

Years later, Eben used to tell me how excited and nervous he was, that first day he was in business for himself. We used to sit late over the coffee and the cheese, and he would smile sympathetically, remembering the youth who tumbled out of bed when midnight was only three hours old—and who hurried down to open his store, to be on time for customers from the early packets coming into the harbor.

But as early and as eager as he was that day, there was one other person in Boston who was ahead of him. That was a little girl named Louisa Bareiss, who had developed a child's innocent liking for the young man from Maine.

Louisa somehow had persuaded her parents to let her hurry down to Eben Jordan's new store that frosty morning in order to be his first customer. And Eben found her there waiting, shivering in the cold darkness, when he arrived to slip the lock.

It was always one of his favorite tales, to recall how proudly she stepped inside, clutching a few coppers in her mittened hand. After careful thought—as becomes a lady shopper—she made her selection.

One yard of cherry-colored ribbon—that was Louisa's purchase. And that one yard of cherry-colored ribbon was the first piece of goods ever sold by Eben Jordan in the city of Boston.

(They tell me the retail sales for 1950 approximated $80,000,-

000 including several miles of cherry-colored ribbon. Eben would have been astonished.)

"I was as happy and proud, selling that ribbon to Louisa, as she was in buying it," Eben used to tell me over our cups.

That, then, was Eben Jordan before I knew him—a man whose family name had been in America since the Rev. Robert Jordan stepped off the boat in 1640—a man descended from the English merchants of Dorsetshire and Devonshire—a man whose father Ebenezer left nine sons and daughters in the state of Maine, along with a family motto that declared, "As for me and my house, we will serve God!" and a man whose greatest thrill in life at the age of 19 was the sale of one yard of cherry ribbon to a shivering little girl.

He and I met 10 years later. We shook hands for the first time on January 20, 1851, when Eben went into partnership with Benjamin L. Marsh. And that was the day that linked the two names that now stand joined on the top deck of New England's greatest department store.

Our home was a shop at 129 Milk Street. Our capital was $5000. Our platform was Eben's principle of trading, that "The better you serve your customers, the better you serve yourself." Our name was Jordan and Marsh.

I didn't mind their leaving me out of the company's name. I knew I was as much a part of the business as their own hearts. They knew it too, and used to consult me on every transaction they made—even though sometimes they didn't realize it themselves. That's one of the satisfactions of being The Observer, the spirit of New England's Jordan Marsh—I can enjoy the romance and the drama of the business without having to make any speeches or otherwise push myself into the public's path.

The following year we took Charles Marsh and one or two others into the firm, and changed the name to Jordan Marsh and Company. That is a particularly important entry because to this very day the extending of that partnership to a Company has invited the Boston boys to enter and seek their future to the mutual gain of all.

Another important move was the fact that Eben and I went to sea in 1853 and made a long, wave-tossed voyage to Europe.

I remember him talking it over with me before we sailed. We were having tea and Indian pudding in his room one night, and he told me what his plans were.

"My friend," he mused, "we're not moving ahead fast enough. We need to expand."

I nodded and helped myself to another dish of pudding, waiting for him to go on.

"By that," he said, "I mean we should expand our line—offer greater selections to our customers—offer them the best products of the European markets—stock our shelves with articles that are strange to these parts.

"Just think," he went on. "There's the whole world to choose from—dolls from Bavaria, linens from Ireland, silks from France, and fine woolens from the Scots lands."

"That will take money," I suggested, a remarkably innocuous observation.

"I don't think it will," Eben replied. He got to his feet. "Pack your bags, Friend Observer," he told me. "We'll set sail for Europe tomorrow—and somewhere over there, I'll find a man who will arrange for me to get my foreign stock on credit."

I had my doubts about that, but being a lover of sea travel on the one hand and an admirer of Eben on the other, I was eager to go along.

Eben found his man without much trouble. He found him in the person of the senior partner of a conservative English commission house. To this day, I believe, the English gentleman was swept off his feet by Eben's fast talk and barrage of arguments—a combination that made such excellent logic that the Englishman could do little but nod his head and gulp inside his high starched collar.

To make it brief, Eben sailed back to Boston with an enormous credit line at his disposal—all obtained without a shilling's worth of backing. It was an astounding piece of business . . . and probably the most amazed man in London was the English businessman who had approved and executed the entire agreement.

I always liked that about Eben. Once he was convinced that an idea of his was sound and honest, he could out-talk a Daniel Webster in getting it into practice. I saw him do it on many and varied occasions.

As it turned out scarcely four years later, that trip to Europe probably was all that saved Jordan and Marsh from a swift exit from the business world—and myself from an early demise as an accredited Observer.

For in 1857, along came a terrible business panic.

Stores collapsed like houses built of cards. Bank accounts vanished like water down a sink. Cherry ribbon became a luxury. It was rough going, and I must admit that there were many sleepless nights when I wondered about Eben's chances of pulling through.

Eben too had sleepless nights, not so much from worry as from staying awake and planning how best to pilot his ship through the stormy seas of tottering finances.

Finally, he made his decision. He told me about it one twilight, as we were walking across Boston Common, trying to air the day's dust from our tired minds.

"The people are not buying," he said. "They want our goods and they need our goods—but they're afraid to spend their money."

I gave a sad nod. I knew he was right.

"As a result," he pointed out, "we're not making sales. If we don't make sales, we'll have to go out of business."

"Very good logic," I remarked.

He snorted. "It's simple arithmetic," he corrected me.

"And what do you intend to do?" I asked him.

"Persuade the people to start buying again." He tossed a nut to a squirrel that scampered across our path.

"Is it that simple?" I asked.

"Yes," he said. "I'll mark everything down to half price. They're afraid to buy now—but when they see the things they need, priced at half what they're worth, nothing in the world can keep them out of the stores—panic or no panic—and especially the ladies."

"And who takes the loss?" I asked, knowing exactly what he would say.

"We'll take it ourselves," he declared, "and hope and pray that the panic will be ended before we reach the point where we can't take it any more. Meanwhile, with whatever comes in, we'll try to keep our credit in good standing."

And that's the way it was, as daring a way of beating a depression as anyone could dream up out of sleepless nights and pots of strong tea. He could have stepped out of business right then, and probably pocketed a comfortable profit. But he was electing to stay in business and watch his capital dwindle by the hour, in order to keep faith with the public and the creditors and with his own self respect.

I halted right there in the middle of Boston Common and jabbed him with my pipe.

"Eben," I told him, "I admire you as a man of courage and grit. If you'll step into that tavern over yonder, I'd like to buy you a noggin and toast your good intentions."

"I'm sorry, my friend," he said, abruptly turning away. "I haven't the time. I'll have to hurry back to the store and start marking the new price tags."

And that's exactly what he did, and exactly how he licked the

Panic of 1857. From that day on, for weeks to come, he took a loss that averaged $3000 a day. But in taking that loss, he held his customers and his creditors—he paid his bills and kept his stock in good shape.

And when the last cloud of the panic vanished, and the sun of prosperity began to rise again, Eben had his store intact and even had a few dollars left in his sock with which to get started again in the new business era that was beginning.

He received many a clap on the back, for the courageous thing he had done. But nothing pleased him more than a letter that came from overseas, from the gentleman in London who had backed his credit line four years earlier.

"Mr. Jordan," the Englishman wrote, "you ought to have a monument to your pluck in preferring honor to profits."

I thought that was a splendid gesture. So did Eben.

Once the panic was over and gone, Eben and his partners stepped ahead with speed. They felt that nothing could stop them now. They moved into larger quarters and built their stock to proportions they'd not have dreamed of five years earlier.

They led the way into new lines of goods, just as the company is doing today. It was a time of change and of fast development. It was a good time to be alive.

But of all the things that happened during that first decade, probably nothing was more important than an incident that escaped virtually everybody's attention.

That was the acquiring of the services of a certain 14-year-old errand boy.

The lad became an entry on Eben Jordan's payroll in 1861, when the company purchased a new piece of property on Washington Street. The property was the retail dry goods store of George W. Warren and Company.

The errand boy, who sort of went with the sale, was a London-born lad named Edward J. Mitton.

I might add that his grandson is Edward R. Mitton, the president of Jordan Marsh today.

CHAPTER II

# THE HOMES I'VE KNOWN

I LAY awake late last night, enjoying the pleasant comfort of my new home at Summer and Chauncy Streets.

You know all about that place, I'm sure. Many of you stood on the sidewalks and watched with me during the long months while the steel girders were going into place and the thousands of red bricks were adding another touch of New England architecture to the beauties of Boston.

You know it for what it is, the first of five new units that one day soon will make the home of Jordan Marsh Company the finest department store in the world.

And many of you who watched the building take shape were on hand with me on the 21st of May, 1949, when Edward R. Mitton stepped forward as president of the company and laid the cornerstone. And if any of you noticed a particularly whimsical expression on my face at that moment, I was only trying to imagine what Edward Mitton's grandfather—the errand boy of 1861— would have thought of the ceremonies.

That was a great day in my life, the day the new cornerstone was laid. It was a great day, too, in the life of Boston and of all New England.

I'll never forget the words of congratulation from President Truman in the White House at Washington.

"It must be quite obvious to all the good people of New England," he wrote, "that this is, indeed, a demonstration of your faith in the future of our Country and your Commonwealth and City."

Majority Leader of the House, Congressman John W. McCormack, who was on hand as the President's representative, told me later that this was the first letter of its kind President Truman ever had written. Then in a speech of his own, the Congressman added:

"We are thankful that the officials of this company have vision to look ahead—to see that New England will, as in the past, continue to live as a leader of our great country."

My friend Senator Leverett Saltonstall was there that day also, and gave an outstanding speech. At one point he summed up the whole situation in five words by declaring:

"This is an historic moment."

I'll always remember those words—and the thousands upon thousands of friends who crowded close to watch the ceremonies —and the television and radio crews on hand to broadcast the event—and the newsmen who wrote about it in their papers.

And as I say, I lay awake in that new abode last night enjoying its pleasant comfort. And I couldn't help smiling in the darkness, looking back across the shadows of 100 years and remembering the other domiciles I'd shared with the Jordan Marsh Company.

My thoughts went all the way back to the beginning, to the little wholesale house we occupied at 129 Milk Street. That was where Eben Jordan and Benjamin Marsh and I first got together, to start the long journey that has brought me here today.

13

In comparison to the stores of modern times, I suppose that Milk Street building wasn't much to talk about. But it was home and it was a starting place, and if sometimes I had to sleep under the counters and eat my supper in one of the stock rooms—well, I didn't mind. It was all a part of growing up.

I suppose if you had told any of us in those days about the wonders of 20th century merchandising, we'd have stared at you with amused derision. We'd never have believed there could be such things as air freight deliveries or air conditioning or electric stairways—or any of the almost incredible things that we take for granted in our business today.

Back in those years Eben was just beginning to grow those unique sideburns of his. I can just imagine how impatiently he'd have tugged at them if anybody had loitered in the Milk Street store long enough to talk about such fantastic creations as module lighting or television sets. Possibly he'd have ordered them out in a rage, indignant that any man should believe him gullible enough to swallow such yarns.

Still, he had vision. Even if he couldn't have imagined the scientific and mechanical wonders that were yet to come, at least he could—and did—foresee that his company was destined to grow and to need larger homes as the years went on. I appreciated that, for my quarters became more comfortable every time we moved.

14

We'd been at Milk Street scarcely five years, when he brought up the subject one night during a quiet stroll along the waterfront. There was a soft east wind that evening, and the smell of salt was in the air. The ships that were moored along the sea wall rode gently on the tide.

Eben had been wordless for a long time, as we'd walked beside the water. I knew there was something on his mind, but I was content to suck my pipe in silence and wait his utterance.

"We're going to need more space, Observer," he said at last.

I nodded and waited for him to go on.

"We're a young company," he continued, "but it's clear already—either we expand now and keep growing, or we stop where we are and live out our lives in a stifling circle. As for me, I choose to expand."

"And where are we going?" I asked him, knocking my pipe on a hitching post.

"There's a vacancy on Pearl Street," he told me. "It's at numbers 18 and 20—and from the way it looks, it shouldn't be too difficult to expand in both directions when the time comes. As a matter of fact, I've already signed an agreement to take over the property."

That was our first move, our first expansion—the first of many that were to come in the years that stretched toward today.

Looking back now, I can see where there was something symbolic in our approach to the Pearl Street property. As Eben had pointed out, there

was space to expand in either direction . . . and throughout these past one hundred years we have grown and grown and grown. This at times has been somewhat inconvenient and caused a deal of bewilderment on the part of our good friends who come to visit us, but with the new building program, it is obvious that the trend today is to put related merchandise next to each other for the great convenience of those who wish to shop, and as the new units of my new home are completed, this far-seeing plan will be more and more apparent to our visitors.

By 1859, though, we had gone about as far as we could in the Pearl Street space, and it seemed a good idea to move again. And this time, we had our eyes on a new six-story structure in Winthrop Square—a handsome stone building that had been hailed by architects and engineers as one of the finest in the entire nation.

It was a lot of work, toting all our stock and our accounts to the new location. There were days when we were so tired and dusty from the job that we had all we could do to stay awake long enough for a warm eggnog at night. But finally everything was in its new place, and we looked around with our vest buttons ready to pop, we were so proud of what we'd done.

I had to smile, thinking about that last night. Our Winthrop Square home gave us 14,400 square feet of floor space, and today our total establishment covers a vast area of 2,015,071 square feet which approximates fifty acres. Imagine that! from the little store on Milk Street to a size of fifty acres!

We were still in Winthrop Square when the Civil War broke out, and I remember how the hoop-skirted ladies and the top-hatted gentlemen cheered from the street when the first Union war flag went up atop our roof. It made me feel good, to see them so spirited and unafraid—yet, it made me feel sad, to think of the heartaches that were bound to come to many homes. With his usual energy to accomplish things, Eben Jordan opened on the main floor of the store the first recruiting station of the day, and a full score of fellow workers marched gallantly away to the strains of "John Brown's body lies a-mouldering in the grave."

But long before the war was over, we'd expanded once again. As a matter of fact, we made our move when the war was very young—in 1861.

This time, we didn't leave the old premises behind us. We merely added new ones. We kept our wholesale business in the Winthrop Square building and bought the retail business that was running under the name of George W. Warren & Company at 450 Washington Street. And if that street number sounds familiar, it's because we're still using it today.

It was a picturesque old place, that first retail store of ours. It was a rugged brownstone building with a brick mansard. Its windows were arched and keystoned, with columns in between. It looked as strong and durable as Plymouth Rock.

It's pleasant to look back now, and to remember the nightly strolls I used to make around that Washington Street neighborhood. I'd go out on the street and stand for a few minutes in the flickering shadows of the gas lamps and watch the people coming and going—and pausing now and then to peer at our new show windows.

Then I'd amble off toward a narrow little by-way known as

Central Court which ran in at right angles from Washington Street. Central Court used to bound one side of our store, and then make an abrupt turn and form the boundary at the back before coming out again on Avon Street.

It was a quaint old alley, ideal for an evening's stroll. If you were hungry, you could step off the sidewalk and wander into Billy Park's Hotel for a seafood dinner. Billy's place used to be known as "The Home of the Broiled Live Lobster." His servings were so delicious that one mouthful was enough to convince you his lobsters had died with a sea chanty in their throats—and a gay, farewell salute of their claws.

If it was entertainment you wanted, you could leave Billy Park's and step next door, to the foyer of the old Theater Comique. It became the Adelphi later on, and possibly its pit orchestra used to play somewhere near the vicinity of our present toilet goods department.

And behind the Adelphi, if I remember, there used to be the attractive Aquarial Garden, with its piscatorial inhabitants swimming around in a setting of sea ferns. P. T. Barnum later took over the garden and installed a few lions and tigers as side attractions. But to me, the place always remained the home of beautiful fish and swaying water flowers. I think Eben agreed with me on that. He used to like to stop in and watch the sea urchins, but he never could get very enthusiastic about Barnum's man-eating lions.

We had been on Washington Street nine years when our next move came. Very unexpectedly, I might add. It took seed one night in 1870, when the glare of flames suddenly cut the darkness at the old Theater Comique. Fire horses rushed snorting to the scene, and firemen in steaming coats battled the blaze with their axes and hand pumps.

The debris was still smoking, and Eben and I were standing on the sidewalk watching the excitement, when he turned to me with a tug of his whiskers and announced, "I think I'll lease that place. Should be able to get it for a good price right now."

Not that he was trying to take advantage of anybody's misfortune, but his idea made good sense. The owners were eager to do business. Jordan and Marsh needed more space close to the retail store, and here was a chance to get it at a reasonable figure.

The deal went through as soon as the building had been repaired. And a few months later, we hauled everything out of our Winthrop Square building, gave up those premises for good, and installed our entire wholesale business in what had once been a theater.

It's a mighty good thing we made that move when we did, for the following year Boston trembled under the roaring flames of the great fire of 1872. And among the buildings that went crashing down in smoke and sparks was the structure we'd had in Winthrop Square.

For a time we thought our Washington Street store and our Central Court place were going up in flames, too. The fire raged close to the walls, but our fellow workers were out in force—pouring buckets of water over the steaming bricks and slapping wet blankets against the sides of the buildings.

We saved what we owned, at the expense of nothing more serious than upset nerves, tired backs, and a few small blisters. But personally, I swallowed so much smoke that night that I didn't light my pipe again for the next fortnight.

During the years that followed, as our business grew, Central Court was closed and gradually engulfed by our spreading establishment. The same thing began to happen on Avon Street, where private homes and small stores were sold to us one by one.

Finally in 1880 we had a chance to buy the corner of Avon and Washington Streets, a step that carried us to the top of the business peak. We built a handsome tower and installed an outdoor clock, and it gave us as well the name of being the finest and biggest store the world had ever seen.

"Surpassing anything attempted either in New York or Philadelphia," was the way the Boston Post described it in 1884.

From that point on, things moved so fast and so steadily that sometimes I'd stand and gape in awe, marveling that anything so big and impressive could have grown from the sale of one yard of cherry ribbon.

As I lay awake last night, I tried to catalogue all the steps in my mind. To me, they told a tale of the spirit of New England initiative and of the great mutual benefits that can arise when a business firm and a buying public have confidence in each other and try to show their liking for each other.

I remembered the big eight-story white-brick building that we built in 1898, at Avon, Chauncy and Bedford Streets—and the marble-lined subway under Avon Street, that connected the new building with the main store. This was the first subway in Boston, and I used to enjoy going down there in the afternoons, to mingle with the shoppers and listen to their words of praise.

And I remember 1907, the year a disastrous fire leveled several neighboring buildings on Avon Street. We had changed our name to Jordan Marsh Company six years earlier, and under that name we bought the fire-blackened ruins and the charred land and started building a great nine-story structure that had the public catching its breath in astonishment.

The building was completed in 1911. It was connected with the 1898 building, and it went down into the earth to a depth of two stories. Actually, it just about doubled our selling space.

The underground part became our first Basement Store, a complete unit in itself and one that was larger at that time than most of the city department stores in the world.

As the years went on, we expanded still more—adding a piece here, and a piece there. We took over the Shuman Store on Washington Street in 1922, and the big Hovey Company Store in 1925.

To sum it up, as I finally did in my own mind last night, that little establishment at 129 Milk Street has grown and grown and grown, but at heart there has been no fundamental change at all. My home today is identical with my home of 100 years ago . . . in each case, filled with the same friendly hospitality.

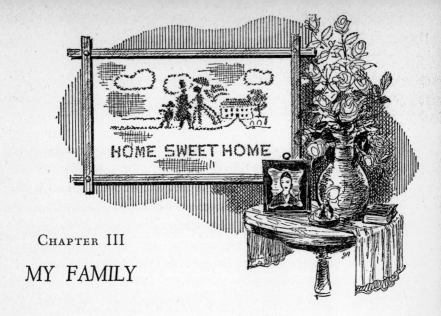

## CHAPTER III

# MY FAMILY

SCARCELY a tick of the clock goes by these days but what some parent from a typical New England home enters one of the Jordan Marsh portals to do some shopping.

I see them coming and I see them going, from the moment the doors open in the morning to the moment when we cover the sales counters for the night. I feel particularly good about it when I see them leaving at twilight with expressions of pleased satisfaction, realizing that they've found exactly what they hoped to buy at exactly the prices they wished to pay.

And as I watch them departing from our store, I find myself daydreaming about their homes and the dear ones waiting their return . . . and I wish for them that happiness which only a home can hold.

Oh, yes, mine, too, has been a happy home. There are more than 7000 fellow workers in our family group, all brought together under one name by those sound policies which were established 100 years ago in the little wholesale store on Milk Street.

Looking back on the growth of our family is one of my favorite

23

recreations these days. I like to sit alone in my new rooms at Summer and Chauncy Streets, and puff at my pipe and remember the names and personalities that have shared our life since 1851. Their descendants and relatives are still by my side, guiding the Jordan Marsh Company along the same sound highway toward new and broader fields.

I've told you much about Eben Dyer Jordan, whose first transaction was the sale of a piece of cherry ribbon now pyramided into one of America's greatest department stores. And I've mentioned his original partner, Benjamin L. Marsh. It was well over half a century ago that the Marsh family dropped from the firm, and the Mitton family stepped to Eben's side.

It was well over half a century ago, too, that Eben Jordan left us.

He was in his 74th year, and the year was 1895, when he passed on. His body lay in state at Trinity Church, and the humble ones and the great ones entered side by side to pay him homage.

On that day I stood off in a corner, half-hidden by the shadows, listening to the things the people said about him.

A little lady with golden hair passed by on her way out, and I heard her say to her companion, "I was one of the 27 buyers he took to Europe 13 years ago. He introduced us to the Lord Mayor of London and to Victor Hugo and to President Grevy of France . . ."

Her voice trailed away at that point, and another took its place. This time the speaker was a man who wore the gold braid of a ship's officer. "We took him across on the Batavia," he was say-

ing. "Monsieur Lafayette . . . the grandson of the Marquis
. . . was forever at his side over there."

An old lady with a shawl on her head came by next, leading a
little boy by the hand. "He helped me to pick out the very coat
you're wearing," she said. "Came right down on the floor with
the sales people, he did, and said he'd guarantee the cloth himself."

There were many who mourned him that day, filing in and out
of the church. I stood there for a long time, alone in the dusk,
and thought how much we were going to miss this man. I'd been
with him when there was only one package of tea in his pantry,
and again when there was thick roast beef on his platter—through
thin times and good. Yes, we would miss him, but I'd remember
particularly one of the last things he'd said to me, just before he'd
passed away.

"My friend," he'd told me, "I'll be leaving you soon, but you
are never to leave the company. You understand that, don't you?
It isn't essential to Jordan Marsh that any one man be its leader
—whether it's Eben Jordan or anybody else. But it is essential
that the company go on to finer things, with always a good leader
as its guide and with other leaders to guide him.

"You understand what I mean by that? I mean that the spirit
of the organization is what counts—and that spirit will outlive
me and those who come after me.

"In other words, my friend," he said at last, "you stay—and as
long as you stay, the Jordan Marsh Company will be what the
people of New England expect it to be. It's the company that
counts, not the individual in the company."

Eben was right! With his passing there came into being a leadership which was one of the most capable combinations ever to tread the path of American merchandising. I'm referring to the team of Eben Jordan, Jr. and Edward J. Mitton.

Young Eben was only 38 years old when he took over his father's role as president. And E. J. Mitton as vice president was 10 years older. As soon as the three of us sat down to discuss plans over a midnight rarebit, I could see that here was a combination that was going to startle the world of retail trade.

They provided a team as nearly perfect as anyone could hope for. Their ideas complemented each other in good old New England fashion, as cranberry sauce adds tang to a turkey dinner or as sleigh bells add liveliness to a sharp winter's night.

Young Eben, with his pince nez and his pointed mustache, was the experimenter—the man who dared to be different. He was a lover of beauty and new ideas, of the unblazed trail and the zest of adventure.

E.J., whose whiskers always made me think of King Edward VII, was the sound conscientious builder . . . a man with both feet on the ground and of straight-hitting action . . . just the man to mold young Eben's dreams into practical business advantages.

The things they did between them are still being felt in the world of merchandising today. Many a store owner, both here and abroad, used to fling up his hands in astonishment, on hearing of the latest innovation being tested at Jordan Marsh Company in Boston. But as sure as snow in winter, those same store owners within a year or so would be adopting the same innovation themselves and wondering why they hadn't thought of it first.

The pair had grown up in Jordan Marsh together, since the days when E.J. had been an errand boy for the old Warren Com-

pany. From errand boy, he had climbed the steps to silk salesman, silk buyer, wholesale business director, member of the firm
and finally vice president. Meanwhile, young Jordan had been
learning the business from his father and had worked at the
counters and in the stock rooms.

The original idea of converting the retail dry goods business
into a department store was young Jordan's, though I seem to remember he had rather a stormy time of it, trying to convince
his father that it was the right thing to do.

Young Eben was always ready to grab his hat and hurry out
the door, in quest of the fruit of a new idea. Many a time I was
weary and out of breath, trying to keep up with him. This amused
him, particularly when he could look at me later in the game
and say with a wry smile, "Well, my friend, we did it again. And
you had your doubts about it, didn't you?"

I certainly did, more times than he knew.

He was a great sportsman and traveler, a connoisseur of the
arts and of cosmopolitan living. One night he decided that Boston should have the best of operatic productions, so he proceeded
to build the Boston Opera House and to run it at his own personal expense for years until it could pay its way alone. Another
night, he was remembering his father's work in helping to found
the New England Conservatory of Music, so he proceeded to
build a new auditorium for the conservatory, thus giving Boston
its famous Jordan Hall.

He ran his own kennels and stables, and gave New England
the best in blue-ribbon horses and thoroughbred dogs. These
hobbies gave him the inspiration to install new departments in
the Jordan Marsh store, one which specialized in the sale of riding habits and another in accessories for dogs. These were abso-
lutely unheard-of in the world of merchandising, but they proved
successful—and it is interesting to note that the Empress Eugenie

of Austria sent to the Jordan Marsh Company in Boston to have made for her a velvet riding habit of rich hunting green!

On another occasion, he decided it might be a good idea to bring great works of art to a place where the shopping public could see them. I'll admit I was aghast at that, when I walked into the main store one day and found him directing the installation of a magnificent art exhibition. The public greeted this with enthusiasm—a fact he never allowed me to forget.

Meanwhile, E.J. was almost constantly at his side, tempering the experiments with practical business sense and from time to time proposing revolutionary ideas of his own.

E.J., for instance, was the first in the merchandising world to try doing business on the "Customer-is-always-right" policy. When it worked, everybody else adopted it. And E.J. was also the first to start selling to retail customers on credit, and to tell them, "If you don't like it—if it isn't exactly what you want—bring it back and get your money back."

Ideas like these jolted the department store operators from Boston to Berlin. They watched in wonderment, positive that such policies would never work—quick to predict bankruptcy and ultimate ruin for "that unusual Jordan Marsh Company." But they were just as quick to pick up the policies for themselves, when they discovered that the team of Jordan and Mitton knew what they were doing.

It was an exciting life, while those two ran the business. They kept me on the move so much that sometimes I couldn't remember whether I'd left my pipe in the new art gallery or my spyglass

in the new Basement Store—or both items in the cabin of an eastbound steamship.

But all such combinations come to an end, sometimes to be replaced by others just as good. E.J. passed on in 1913, shortly after he had served as president during a two-year illness that afflicted his friend Eben. And Eben Jordan, Jr. himself died only three years later.

After they'd gone, I walked through the store for a while, examining some of the improvements they'd brought to Jordan Marsh. The list was like a page from a chronicle of mechanical progress—telephones, glass show cases, electric lights, pneumatic cash circuits, fire alarm boxes, elevators. Together they'd been quick to see whatever was new and good, and to adapt it to Jordan Marsh. They had made our company New England's fastest-growing business.

You'd think that the passing of such a pair would have had a crippling effect on a firm like Jordan's. But as old Eben had told me years before, "The spirit of the organization is what counts."

That spirit, then, was seized and carried on by E.J.'s son, George W. Mitton, my very close friend, who assumed our presidency in 1916.

As I watched G.W. continue the fine policies of other years, I noticed that he also brought to Jordan's many good innovations of his own which have been copied by other companies through the years.

George W. Mitton was a great hu-

manitarian. He had a heart as warm as the sun and as kind as the touch of a loving father. I first met him when he came to Jordan's in 1888, as an 18-year-old stock boy in the wholesale department. With time, he had gone on the road as a traveling salesman, had supervised the buying of wholesale dress goods, and eventually had moved into the main office in charge of merchandising.

It was G.W. who told me that in his opinion it was against the principles and spirit of Jordan's to maintain one group known as employers and another group known as employees. He had been president only a little more than a year, when he announced there'd be a change.

"Hereafter," he declared, "there'll be no such thing as a Jordan's employee. From here on, we're all fellow workers regardless of our position with the company."

And that's the term that's been in use ever since. It's a term I particularly like for it symbolizes the side-by-side workmanship and spirit that built New England—that started with a tiny cluster of cabins on a bleak stretch of shore and brought us all to the greatness that we know today.

G.W.'s sympathies were always with the fellow workers and the friends who came to buy. He established the credit union, to help the workers over their financial bumps. He was the first to install free medical and dental care, and to keep a staff of nurses on hand for emergency treatment.

He conceived and set up the first Executives' Training Course in the history of retail trade, declaring that Jordan's should train its own future officers and should promote from within whenever possible. This worked out so well that there's scarcely a major business in the world today that hasn't followed the same plan.

When G.W. stepped out of the presidency in 1930, and

moved to the position of chairman of the board of directors, he was followed by his brother Richard as president—a man who in many respects was like Eben Jordan, Jr. By that I mean that Richard Mitton was a perfectionist—a good mixer—a cooperative partner. I often thought I detected a great similarity between the teamwork of the two brothers, and the teamwork that had been shown earlier by young Eben and E. J. Mitton.

And as always, I could see again where old Eben had been right in declaring that, "The spirit of the organization is what counts." Good men and good leaders had come and gone since the night he'd spoken those words, and in no case had any one of them tried to elevate himself above the welfare of the company. Each one had considered the company first, with the result that it grew stronger and more progressive as the years passed along.

So it was when Edward R. Mitton stepped into the presidency in 1937, and so it remains today. I had watched Edward Mitton enter the business as G.W.'s son, coming directly from the classrooms of Harvard.

He was born on June 21, 1896, in the town of Brookline, where he still makes his home. Before entering Harvard, he attended Milton Academy.

He joined the Jordan Marsh Company on October 1, 1917, starting work as a sales clerk behind a counter. He left the store to serve his country in the Navy and upon his return he rose to executive capacity through the roles of auxiliary merchandiser, divisional merchandise manager and general merchandise manager, becoming a director of the corporation on April 17, 1924, and merchandising vice president on July 30, 1931. After 25 years of service, he was elected a member of the company's Quarter Century Club with the Class of 1942. Throughout his association with the company, he has preserved the good traditions of his forebears—pride in the organization, warmed by a determination to keep the best of old qualities alive.

I must say that my close association with Edward these days has further strengthened my opinion that here then is the second great builder of this organization's history. For it was he that planned the construction of the bridge across Avon Street to the Annex, back in the late 'teens, in such a manner that it would stand unsupported by itself when and if a new building were to be erected some day, and thus the way was paved for the present new building operations without interruption of traffic flow to and from the Annex.

Furthermore, it has been his clear vision and forceful determination which has brought about the great new construction era which inaugurates this turn of the Jordan Marsh century. In other words, his policy has been that the best of the old must be continued and embodied in the new.

That brings us to my 100th birthday, then, and to the other officers of the company who assist Edward R. Mitton in the administration of the business. In a way, you would call them an all-New England team, for if there's a trace of outside influence in any of them, it has long since been adapted to the spirit of New England progress and initiative.

In charge of the merchandise division of the management is Cameron S. Thompson, vice president and general merchandising manager. Born in Syracuse, N. Y., September 3, 1898, he came to New England at a young age. He was graduated from Tufts College in 1921, and went to work for Jordan Marsh that July as a stock boy in the rug department. He completed the Executive Training Course, became a buyer, merchandise manager of the Street Floor, and then vice president in 1937, and is

Edward R. Mitton

Cameron S. Thompson

Robert Mitton

Richard H. Edwards, Jr.

William A. Everett

James H. Fairclough, Jr.

now a member of the Quarter Century Club. His home is on Joy Street in Boston.

Assisting in the merchandising of this great store is Robert Mitton, brother of the company's president, who also holds the position of vice president and assistant general merchandising manager. Born in Brookline September 15, 1900, he attended Noble and Greenough School before entering Harvard. He came to the organization November 7, 1922, and worked at first in the planning department. He became a director of the company on April 3, 1934, and a vice president on April 24, 1944. He is now a member of the Quarter Century Club and lives on St. Paul Street in Brookline.

Richard H. Edwards, Jr., the vice president in charge of sales, promotion, and publicity was born in Boston March 19, 1901, and went from the Brookline public schools to Wesleyan University in Connecticut. He entered the Executive Training Course in 1922, rose to Buyer, and then to Merchandise Manager of the Men's and Boys' division. He was elected a director of the company in 1942, and vice president in May 1943. He, too, is a member of the Quarter Century Club, since 1947. His present home is in Concord.

The treasurer and vice president in charge of non-merchandising activities is William A. Everett. Born in Charlestown January 21, 1897, he attended the public schools of Everett and Northeastern University. He became a member of the Quarter Century Club in 1936 and was elected a vice president in 1937. His home is in Winchester.

James H. Fairclough, Jr., vice president in charge of personnel, was born in Boston May 2, 1894, and educated in the schools of Cambridge. He entered the company in 1916, became a member of the Quarter Century Club in April, 1942, and was elected a

34

vice president in May 1943. His home is on Forest Avenue, West Newton.

Working close by the side of these men are two other company officers, Assistant Treasurer Howard W. Davis of Waban and Assistant Clerk Charles L. H. Carle of Malden.

The president and five vice presidents all are members of the Board of Directors. The other directors of the company are Edward J. Pendergast of West Newton, Adolph Ehrlich of Brookline, Walter M. Stone of Newtonville, Newton L. Walzer of Milford, N. H., Isadore Jacobson of Brookline, B. Earl Puckett and Arthur C. Hallan.

That, then, is the administrative team which works today with the 7000 fellow workers in carrying on the tradition of the sale of cherry ribbon. It's a team that old Eben Jordan himself would have enjoyed working with, for its guide and its pride lie deep within the reality of Eben's fondest hope:

"The spirit of the organization is what counts most."

## Chapter IV

# THE WAY WE LIVE

As OFTEN as time permits these days, I stroll through the aisles and showrooms of Jordan Marsh, listening to the comments of our friends, the shoppers.

It's a quiet and instructive bit of recreation, ideal for one of my longevity and nature. Also, it has a very practical side, too, for sometimes an astute visitor, looking at Jordan's objectively, can see opportunities for improving our services—opportunities that may have missed the attention of those of us so close to the business.

For that reason, I always keep my ear tuned in the hope of picking up some helpful hint—something that might aid us still more in striving to make Jordan's the favorite store for all New England.

Perhaps I've stood at your very elbow while you've shopped— or perhaps I've ridden with you in the elevators.

Incidentally, just the other day, I heard one lady saying to another, "You know, one reason I always enjoy shopping at Jordan's is because the sales people are so friendly. They seem to like their

36

work—to be happy in what they're doing, and somehow they relay that pleasant feeling to the customers. That makes shopping here a pleasure."

Of course, it gave me a warm glow to hear that. In fact, I went straight to my room and began polishing my spyglass—a chore which I usually find monotonous after 100 years, and one which I always postpone as long as possible.

While I was rubbing the brasswork with my polishing cloth, I thought of what that lady in the store had said. I tried to remember all the things we do in Jordan Marsh to make the fellow workers more contented with their lives.

Probably one of the best features of all is the Executive Training Course which was started by George W. Mitton. The very fact that this course is in existence is a challenge to every fellow worker to improve his position through proper application to his duties.

I've told you about the purpose of the course—to train young men and women for the executive positions in the store. At least half of the 80 to 100 members who start the course every September are chosen from within the store itself. The other half bring in fresh influences from the graduating classes of colleges or equivalent educational backgrounds.

The course runs for two years, and during that time the members work throughout the store on a rotation plan—from receiving room to warehouse, from credit office to sales counter, from inventory to advertising, and so it goes.

Meanwhile, they attend instruction classes, listen to lectures, conduct panel discussions, study films on salesmanship and receive their education through these channels—plus serving the public as they learn.

You can imagine what two years of that sort of thing does for a person. It gives one a knowledge of Jordan's that never could

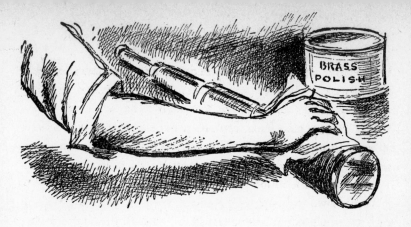

be acquired in any other way—and it fits one for promotion to that higher position when a vacancy occurs. In this way, Jordan Marsh builds most of its best executive ability right within its own walls.

Besides this, the Training Department is always actively on the lookout for workers of unusual talents. This is the department that helps to mould the new fellow workers in those roles which will qualify them for better positions. Here is the place where one will study those special courses in merchandising, speech, salesmanship, fashions—and all sorts of allied subjects.

Naturally, the benefits of such courses are reflected by the improvement in a person's work—and in turn, assist to make shopping a pleasure at Jordan's.

I should have asked that lady in the store if she had any particular person in mind when she spoke of friendly sales people. The thought occurred to me that she might have been talking that very morning with somebody who had just been admitted to membership in the Half Century Club or the Quarter Century Club. Admission to either of these clubs always cloaks the new member in a special veil of good spirits.

The Half Century Club was founded on January 15, 1922, when George W. Mitton was president of the company. More than 100 persons have been admitted since its origin—100 members, each of whom has spent at least 50 years as a Jordan Marsh fellow worker.

New members are taken in every year at an annual banquet. When joining the Club, they are given a check for $1000 and an emblematic platinum pin studded with diamonds. Today, 54 active members welcome the newcomers yearly to their ranks.

The Quarter Century Club is much larger, of course. When it was founded in January 1919, there were 201 charter members, each of whom could look back on 25 years with the company. Incidentally, Calvin Coolidge was governor of Massachusetts when this club began, and attended the charter meeting as the guest of honor.

Going on into clubs of another sort, brings up the matter of cash and credit. They say no family is a happy one if it's bothered with too many financial problems, so here at Jordan's we've tried to smooth out some of the financial bumps that sooner or later jar almost everybody.

For one thing, we have our voluntary Association for Mutual Aid which was organized back in 1905.

It's just what the name implies—an association for mutual aid. All the members pay weekly dues, in ratio to their wages. Then if and when illness comes along, they draw their benefits.

Another avenue of help for the fellow workers lies in the Jordan Credit Union, which has been in operation now since 1931.

This outfit was organized under the banking laws of Massachusetts to offer small loans at reasonable interest rates. Since it came into being, fellow workers have borrowed some $2,000,000 from its cash drawer. Its assets today are close to $700,000. It is operated strictly without profit and belongs exclusively to the people, and not to the company.

In addition, the company encourages savings through the popular Christmas Clubs and Vacation Clubs.

And speaking of vacations, every fellow worker with a year of service on his record gets a two-week vacation with pay in the summer, and can look forward to even better vacations in the years ahead. After five years with the company, there's an extra one-week vacation in the winter—and this becomes a two-week winter vacation after 10 years.

Meanwhile, the company insures entirely at its own expense all full-time fellow workers with over three years of service, covering them with

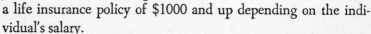

a life insurance policy of $1000 and up depending on the individual's salary.

Another thing that makes shopping a pleasure at Jordan's is the healthy condition of the men and women who meet the public. Yet, probably not one shopper in 100 knows about the medical staff that is at work behind the scenes.

The company maintains a modern Health Department located in the Bristol Building, as well as first aid rooms in the Main Buildings and at the Cambridge Service Station.

A physician, a dentist, a chiropodist and a dental hygienist are always on duty, and besides these there are five registered nurses and one practical nurse. One of the registered nurses, incidentally, also serves as a visiting nurse and uses a company automobile to make visits to the homes of fellow workers when they're taken ill.

Of course, there's more to health than pills and doctors, and has been since mankind first learned to complain about headaches. And there too, the Jordan policy is to help the fellow worker stay healthy through relaxation and recreation.

For relaxation, there is a well-stocked library and reading room on the ninth floor of the Annex. I frequently go there myself, to keep up with the best in modern literature and also to browse among the old books that Eben used to read.

Sometimes, too, while I'm on that floor I stop in for a quiet game of solitaire and a smoke in the Men's Game Room. There's always a checker bout going on, or a round of gin rummy. And just across the way, there's a comfortable lounge for the ladies— a spot where they can relax and chat and listen to a little music.

These rest rooms, by the way, are sometimes the scene of some first class Monday-morning quarterbacking—as to why Joe Whoozits won the annual golf tournament—and why the Braves or Red Sox ought to get a new pitcher—and what's the word on the bowling teams.

Whether it's athletics or a game of canasta, it's all part of a good health program—and it's one more reason why Jordan's is a good place to shop.

These are just a few of the advantages of being a fellow worker in the place I call my home. There are many others—like the fellow-worker discount on anything bought in the store—and the charge accounts for workers and their dependents—and the big cafeteria, and the special rates in certain departments, and the friendliness of the personnel counsellors. And so it goes—and if I've missed many points, sooner or later you'll run across them in the columns of The Tally, our monthly store-wide newspaper.

And above everything else, of course, comes the customer.

It's as true now as it was on the day we began our business on Milk Street—that helpful friendly service is the company's very cornerstone. All else—the benefits for Fellow Workers and all the rest—ultimately are planned to make the customer a satisfied visitor.

With this in mind, Jordan's tells the individual Fellow Worker to, "Be a host to each customer, as you would a guest in your home."

And one night just a short time ago, a new member of our group came to me and asked if I'd explain that more fully—if I'd tell him exactly what the customer should expect in Jordan's. So I told him to sit in my leather chair and help himself to my tobacco, while I tried to put it into words.

"For one thing," I said, pacing slowly up and down, "you should always approach the customer—don't make her approach you. See that her first impression is a good one.

"Then try to capture her point of view. Try to put yourself in the customer's place. Perhaps she doesn't even know what she wants herself—but you, with a little skillful questioning, can learn what's on her mind and help her to decide.

"You should know all there is to know about your merchandise. You should be able to answer whatever question the customer asks, whether it's about the material in the product or the place where it was manufactured.

"You should be enthusiastic in presenting your merchandise—like an enthusiastic host displaying his new ice bucket. Let the

customer handle the articles. Make it apparent that it's a pleasure to be of service. Do you follow me?"

He said he did, so I continued.

"Always keep yourself neat and well-groomed," I went on. "Always be courteous.

"And another thing, don't hesitate to suggest a few related articles that might be bought. Perhaps, in doing so, you'll remind the customer of something he or she intended to buy and had forgotten all about. You'll possibly be saving her another trip to town. She'll appreciate that.

"And always remember to take pride in your work—to be proud of your organization. Your feeling will transmit itself to the customer, who in turn will be proud to say to her friends, 'Oh, yes, I bought that at Jordan's. I do all my shopping there now.'"

My visitor nodded his head. "I see what you mean," he remarked. "I suppose that's the sort of thing one learns after a century in the business."

"It's the sort of thing we teach in Jordan's every day in the year," I corrected him. "We teach it in the training courses and the sales conferences, and we teach it to each other by putting it into daily practice."

We talked for an hour or so longer, my young visitor and myself. I told him the whole history of the store, and of how the company's aim from the very beginning has always been to please the customer.

I told him, too, of how Jordan Marsh and Boston and New England had grown together, side by side, each benefiting the other as the years went by. I spoke of the vision of the Jordan leaders—how the company had served as a springboard for new ideas in merchandising, and in social benefits as well—how the organization was able to move with the times and yet retain a handclasp with the good things of old New England.

43

The shadows in my room were dark and still I talked on, for I saw in this young beginner the symbol of what Jordan's stands for—the symbol of training fellow workers in the Jordan tradition of good service to the customer and loyal pride to the company.

Also, I must confess that when I get started on the subject of the rise of Jordan Marsh, I seldom pay any attention to time. As long as there's a willing listener in front of me, I merely let my story run its course.

At any rate, I like to think I gave my young visitor some valuable points on how to be a good Jordan Marsh representative. I certainly tried to give a clear picture of the way we live and the reason we enjoy our work with the company.

And that's exactly what I've tried to do in these last few pages—to bring the customer behind the scenes at Jordan's and to point out some of the reasons why it's a good place to work and a good place to shop.

Our organizations, our principles, our services, our safety measures—they're all working toward the mutual goal of pleasant relations with our visitors.

It's a good thing to think about, while polishing the brass of an old spyglass. It keeps me content with my lot.

Meanwhile, I have been thinking that perhaps I'll establish another club at Jordan's, to go with the Quarter Century and the Half Century Clubs.

My new organization will be known as the Century Club. It will be extremely exclusive. I will be its charter member and its entire official board.

My membership badge will be a little rosette of cherry ribbon —and my annual banquet will be one cherry pie from the Jordan Marsh bakery department.

CHAPTER V

# THROUGH THE WARS

HERE in New England, we've always been quick to spring to arms to defend our way of life.

It was that way long before we gave birth to our American government. It will remain that way as long as this America exists.

As far back as 275 years ago, our Colonial forebears seized their muskets and their powder horns and followed the command of Captain Ben Church of Duxbury, battling the savage Indian tribes of King Philip in a war that raged all across southern New England. Fire and death nearly wiped out the colonies of Plymouth, Massachusetts, and Providence Plantations in those days—but New England courage pulled the settlers through to victory.

One hundred years later, New Englanders rose again, this time to fight for their independence. They dropped their plows and their hay rakes and hurried toward Lexington and Concord with their muskets in their hands, to give the world a new nation destined to become a great leader.

They fought again in 1812, when their seamen were being

kidnaped from the decks of ships outward bound from Portland and Salem and Boston. And again when Santa Ana came storming north from Mexico, and the call went up for volunteers to journey south and defend our borders.

So it has been, from the days of bows and arrows to the days of stratospheric missiles. New Englanders—always preferring peace to conflict—have yet been quick to seize their guns when war has thrust itself upon them.

I was thinking of our great battle heritage just the other day, when I strolled through the Main Store and paused to watch a shopper studying the names of the Jordan Marsh fellow workers on our World War memorial plaques. Like the spirit of New England itself, the spirit of Jordan's has always been swift to respond to the slogan, "Peace—but not at the price of honor."

That was our feeling in 1861, when the shots rang out that heralded the opening of bitter conflict between the North and the South.

New Englanders did not want that war. And Eben Jordan, as a typical New Englander, watched in helpless sorrow as the battle clouds began to gather.

"There's no avoiding it," he said to me one night, as we walked by twilight along the banks of the Charles River. "War will come as surely as tomorrow's sunrise—and for the sake of a great nation's future, we cannot permit ourselves to be divided. The South and the North must live together as one nation."

We had just heard the news from Fort Sumter that evening. The outlook was discouraging. Conflict at this time seemed certain to rip a young nation apart and to plant seeds of bitterness that might flourish for a half-century or more, whatever the outcome of the battles.

"It will be bad for our business, too," I ventured, wondering

47

how long it would be before we'd again know the
serenity of those evening walks by the riverside.

"Our business from now on is the business of
supporting our country's government," Eben replied. "Anything else is secondary."

"That," I told him, "is exactly what I expected
you to say."

And that was precisely what was in his mind
the next morning, when Jordan Marsh ran aloft
the first flag to be raised in Boston
after the declaration of war.

That flag went up atop our six-
story freestone building in Winthrop Square. The streets and
sidewalks below were jammed
with tight-vested men and their
hoop-skirted ladies, cheering their
hearts out in spirited patriotism.

Simultaneous with the flag-
raising, Eben sent a call to all the

able-bodied men in the store. Jordan Marsh, he announced, would back to the limit any man who would step forth and fight for his country. The company stood ready to buy uniforms for all the volunteers. Every man rallying to his flag would get his full salary for as long as he stayed in the army—and would find his job waiting for him when the din of battle ended.

What's more, Eben told them, Boston's first recruiting station was hereby declared in operation on the ground floor of the Jordan Marsh Company—and the best sign of a man's patriotism would be the speed with which he could get to the desk and sign up.

I was standing in an unfortunate position when this announcement was made. I was too close to the desk itself. I was nearly bowled off my pins by an onrush of 48 young men, hurrying to get their names on file for the blue of the Union Army. The first rush knocked my spyglass out of my hands and put a dent in its brasswork that's still there to this day.

New England responded as I knew it would. Uncertainty was swept away, and men marched forth in stout-hearted files, eager to don their country's uniform and fight for the integrity of their nation.

Eben himself took over the leadership of the Sanitary Commission, forerunner of the American Red Cross.

There's no point in going into the hardships and cruelties of the long embattled years that followed. It was probably the saddest chapter in our nation's history—but one which would have been even more sorrowful if men like our young New Englanders had not held the country together at the cost of their own blood.

Those years of pain and trouble had a harsh effect even upon New England homes that had been spared the loss of a husband, son or brother. For one thing, there were many families that depended on companies like Jordan Marsh for their household

49

supplies. And as time crept on and the war still raged, they found that the lines of battle were cutting critical gaps across the lines of trade.

I saw this condition taking shape, and wondered apprehensively just what could be done to change it. Of course, the swiftest way to improvement would be an early victory by the Union armies—but that, for a time, appeared to be a goal almost beyond reach.

What I didn't realize was that another friend of Eben Jordan's also had been combing his brain for a solution to this problem.

The friend I speak of was a young man of 27 when the war broke out—a man of initiative and daring and keen imagination. He had come down from Bennington, Vt., to take a job with Eben's company, and he had risen to an official position by the time this dilemma became serious.

His name is well known on the pages of American finance— Jim Fisk.

I remember vividly the night Jim told us his plans. He and Eben and I sat in a downtown hotel room, looking over the latest reports from the battlefields. They were not encouraging.

"Mister Jordan," said Fisk, biting an unlighted cigar, "we can't go on this way much longer—the North, I mean."

"What are you getting at?" asked Eben, still keeping his eyes on a news dispatch.

"New Englanders are counting on this company to stay alive —but the company may have to go out of business if the North is defeated," Fisk said bluntly. "The North cannot win without gunpowder. Gunpowder cannot be made without cotton—and all the cotton is in the South."

"So?" said Eben, raising his head.

"So the answer to everything is to get the cotton out of the South and bring it north," Fisk declared.

"You make it sound easy," Eben replied. "Do you know of any way to bring cotton north?"

"Yes," said Jim Fisk. "I can arrange it."

Eben stared at him wordlessly for a few minutes. I probably gave him a startled glance myself.

Fisk leaned across the table and spoke in earnest tones.

"Look, Mister Jordan," he said, "I can't get enough cotton north to supply the whole Union army and neither could any other individual. But I can get big quantities here—and perhaps when they see me doing it, other men will try the same scheme.

"In time," he declared, "we can get a steady flow of cotton— enough to make all the gunpowder we need to win the war."

"Tell me what you're planning," Eben said quietly.

"I have a lady friend in the South," Fisk disclosed. "I'd rather keep her name out of it. But she's in a position to control the movement of hundreds of bales of cotton—possibly thousands.

"Also, I have friends who tell me they know the weak spots in the Confederate lines—not only on land, through the woods and valleys, but also at sea, straight through the blockade.

"What I propose is this: Give me your support and let me make all the arrangements with the Federal Government and with my informants. I'll guarantee to smuggle a mountain of cotton from the South. That's all, Mister Jordan."

Eben regarded him narrowly for a moment or two and then nodded abruptly. He held out his hand to seal the agreement. "Go ahead, Mister Fisk," he said. "Make the proper contacts—and I'll respect any confidence you place in me."

And that's how it happened, that from an informal meeting in a Boston hotel room, the hands were set in motion that were to cut holes in the Confederate blockade. Before long, in the dark nights that followed, mule trains loaded with contraband cotton were rumbling over the rutted secret roadways that led through the Southern lines—and on the blacked-out ocean, swift schooners were running the seaborne blockade.

Cotton began to move northward—and other enterprising men began to follow Jim Fisk's daring plan—and the stockpiles of gunpowder for the Union troops began to mount to formidable heights.

After what seemed like an eternity of grief, at long last the final shot was fired. We accepted the hard-earned triumph with the rest of the victorious North, prayerfully grateful for the surrender of General Lee at Appomattox—yet saddened and pained that the war had been necessary.

At Jordan Marsh, we welcomed back the men who had marched away and who had survived the horrors of Cold Harbor and Chickamauga and Shiloh. Then we settled down to the business of supporting the economics of a weary, patched-up nation. We were still much too close to the war itself to give vent to a joyous, full-hearted celebration.

A few years later, however, the sounds of battle were far enough behind us to justify the glorious crescendo of a stirring chorus of thanksgiving.

It took the form of the great National Peace Jubilee of 1869, one of the most rousing events ever to thrill the heart of Boston. Eben Jordan and Patrick Sarsefield Gilmore were the forces behind this show—Gilmore the promoter, the organizer, the cheer-leader—Jordan the backer and the financial director.

Together they built a mammoth coliseum, about where Trinity Church now stands. They built it big enough to seat 50,000 people in the audience, crowding shoulder to shoulder to hear 10,000 others raise their voices in triumphant song.

The flames of 2400 gas tapers sputtered and flared above the upraised faces of the huge crowd, as the strongest and truest singing voices in America crashed into stirring chords of harmony. Thousands of musicians supported the jubilee songs with their trumpets and drums. And even before the last notes died away on the night wind, Eben Jordan was hurrying to Pat Gilmore's side with enthusiastic plans for a jubilee that would be even greater—the Gigantic International Music Festival of 1872.

That was an event which probably never has been equalled in the musical history of the world, and may never again be approached. It makes my pulse jump even now, just to remember the way that music thundered across the skies of Boston.

For that 1872 festival, Gilmore and Eben Jordan enlarged their flag-decked coliseum, and they brought to Boston the best of European music masters to make the rafters tremble.

Ranking choral clubs, choirs and soloists from all over America streamed into the city to join their colleagues from overseas in a gigantic glee club that topped 20,000 voices.

Celebrated bands from England, Ireland, France and Germany joined a 1000-piece American orchestra for the overtures and background music.

Johann Strauss, in demand at virtually every court in Europe, deserted his home continent and arrived in Boston at the head of his own Austrian orchestra. From the moment the first strains of the "Beautiful Blue Danube" poured forth, he had the city waltzing in a whirl of lilting happiness.

For twenty consecutive days and nights, the festival drew crowds from all corners of the lands, with travelers arriving by rail, steamboat, foot and horseback.

President Ulysses S. Grant—fresh in the minds of the crowds as the victorious Yankee general—came and acknowledged the rocking cheers with waves of his tall silk topper.

Madame Minna Peschka-Leutner, the "Leipsig Nightingale," sang with the voice that had thrilled the richest audiences of Europe. From Germany came the "Kaiser's Own" cornet quartet, with the world famous Herr Saro as solo trumpeter. From Paris came the renowned Garde Republicaine Band, to give a crashing performance of "John Brown's Body" in the mistaken belief that this was the American national anthem. And from London came the celebrated Grenadier Guards Band, an organization that won my admiration for its music but also my sympathy for its discomfort—as Boston's June sun beat down upon its bearskin shakos.

To top it all—and probably to forge something that will never be equalled in American music—came the two Jordan-Gilmore grand displays.

One of these was the resounding rendition of the Anvil Chorus from Il Trovatore, with Pat Gilmore leading a chorus of 23,000 voices and an orchestra of 1000 instruments—backed up by 100 Boston firemen clanging their mighty hammers on 100 anvils.

The second pièce de résistance was the grand finale presentation of the Star Spangled Banner—with all the above plus the cannonading of 100 pieces of artillery and the rousing chimes of church bells from steeples across the city.

As Oliver Wendell Holmes wrote of it at the time:

> "Let the loud tempest of voices reply,
> Swell the vast song till it mounts to the sky . . ."

I assure you, that's exactly what happened.

That, then, has always been the Jordan Marsh attitude toward war and peace—determined and spirited in support of war, when the nation's life is at stake—strong in its hymn of thanksgiving when peace with honor has again arrived.

That combination of courage and spirit flared again in 1917 when the call to action sounded from the battlefields of Europe.

Now for the first time in history, Americans were being sent abroad to shed their blood on foreign ground. None of us realized it then, but we were entering a new phase of American relations. From that point on, the interests of New England and the rest of the nation were to be inevitably linked with the interests of the world at large. We were stepping forth on our path to global leadership—and Jordan Marsh was quick to answer the call.

Once again, our men donned the uniforms for battle service. Once again the flag of patriotism rippled above our rooftops. The names of 395 fellow workers went up on the plaque that listed those who served.

And when the final shell screamed over No Man's Land on

November 11, 1918, five stars marked the names of the fellow workers who had given their all in their country's service.

It seemed far too short an interlude, before we were once again putting up a plaque. A new one, this time—and a much larger one—and one that marked a longer and bloodier age of warfare. Hitler had broken loose—the Japs had struck at Pearl Harbor—and there was nothing for it but to raise the battle flag again on December 7, 1941.

I took a long walk by myself that night, thinking of the ordeals that our friends beyond the sea had been going through for more than two years. I thought of the armored columns, thundering across the dry plains of Poland—and the screaming Stukas, diving upon the crowded highways of France—and the droning bombers, dropping their tons of death and fire upon the battered cities of England. And though I dreaded the heartaches that would come to New England homes, still I was relieved that the time had come for me to declare myself and to stand beside my faraway friends in the white heat of battle.

One by one, I watched my fellow workers take up their places in the fighting ranks, till at last there were 844 men and women gone from Jordan Marsh. Seven of these were to make the supreme sacrifice before the dawn of peace.

Watching these hundreds go forth, I saw them flung to the far corners of the earth. I saw them sweat through the steaming jungles of Guadalcanal, where snipers perched like monkeys in the treetops. I saw them man their icy deck guns on the North Atlantic, when swarms of submarines struck at our convoy lines. I saw them move from the bitter blows of Kasserine Pass to the boot of Italy, and slowly slug their way north against Kesselring's iron line. I saw them at Normandy—and in the red-painted skies over Berlin—and on the black beach of Iwo Jima. And at that historic battle of the Coral Sea, where the Japanese navy was met and sunk, two planes of the very first flight of bombers were piloted by two men, who as little lads had received their original aeronautic schooling in the Jordan Marsh Junior Aviation Club. These two boys never returned from that first flight, but they will always be flying outward and onward in our most sacred memories.

Oh, yes, I saw our fellow workers, too, strengthening the line at home—doing the monotonous work of administration and supply and finance and morale, where the only glory was the satisfaction in a man's heart that he had been given a job and had done it well.

Jordan's did everything it was called upon to do—and much that was done on its own initiative.

War bond drives were held, with stars of stage, screen and radio on hand to urge the people to back their nation with every dime they could spare.

Jordan's was one of the first stores in the nation to urge its customers to bring in their old furs, and to convert those furs into vest linings for the seamen who were fighting the Battle of the Atlantic.

Jordan's also sent out an appeal for old silk and nylon stockings, to be used in making powder bags for the heavy guns of the Army and Navy. More than 35,000 stockings were brought into the store in answer to this appeal, and one woman alone brought in 1336 stockings she had saved over a period of 25 years to make braided rugs.

Early in 1942, the company sparked one of its war bond drives by calling in a delegation of "Unsung Heroes"—the men who had survived torpedoings on the sub-infested convoy lanes.

Those things were typical of the work being done, but I think one of the most valuable things the organization accomplished was when it issued the Liberty Overseas Editions of the Boston

Herald. Each Monday, Jordan's made 20,000 miniature photostatic copies of that day's Herald and offered them freely for distribution, to be mailed abroad for the morale of those in service. These 20,000 copies were gone regularly by 10 A.M. every Monday, eagerly seized by relatives and friends of somebody in uniform.

Thousands of letters were received at Jordan's, thanking the company for this service and adding that this, in many cases, was the only bit of live news that was reaching the theaters of battle, and one such paper was found among the personal effects of a dead Jap in the Aleutian Islands.

Unquestionably one of the finest of all Jordan Marsh contributions in the field of morale was the tremendous "Tribute to the Unconquerables," staged in January 1944 as a launching impetus to the Fourth War Loan Drive.

This great display was sponsored by the company in cooperation with the U. S. Treasury Department and the Saturday Evening Post. Nobody will ever be able to measure the extent of valuable service that it accomplished.

It opened on the night of Saturday, January 8, with a $1000-per-plate banquet in the main ballroom of the Copley Plaza Hotel. I was there that night—and as one who can look back upon 100 years of living, let me say that I never saw anything to equal it.

The ballroom was brilliantly decorated with the flags of all the allied nations. At the head table I recognized such leaders as Major General Sherman Miles, commanding general of the First Service Command; Rear Admiral DeWitt Ramsey, vice chief of the Navy's Bureau of Aeronautics; Charles Francis Adams, former Secretary of the Navy; Leverett Saltonstall, who was then governor of the state; Maurice Tobin, then mayor of Boston; executives of the Jordan Marsh Company, diplomatic representatives, religious leaders, patriots from the world of finance and the world of arts—and it would take far too much space to list all the special guests.

The dinner was a complete sellout, and produced more than $11,000,000 in sales of war bonds.

I remember looking out upon the faces of the listeners when Admiral Ramsey rose to make the feature speech. He told how the Nazi submarines had been beaten back from the blacked-out shores of New England—and of how the Japs had been halted and rocked back on their heels in the Pacific. But I was glad to note that he did not try to deck the picture with pretty promises and too much optimism.

"There is no evidence of deterioration of German fighting morale," he told his listeners. "As we move toward the centers of resistance, the going will get tougher."

I looked at their faces, then—the faces of men and women from England and France, Poland and Norway, and all the other embattled lands. I saw there the thin, humorless smiles of confidence —the same determined expressions I had seen on the faces of potential victors in times of stress before. And I knew that this was what they wanted—to hear the facts, so that they would best know how to finish the fight.

And on the following Monday morning, these men and women and thousands of their comrades brought the "Tribute to the Unconquerables" to its grand climax with one of the most stirring parades the streets of Boston had ever beheld.

I stood that day in the reviewing stand and, passing before me, in the chill bleak air of a New England January, I saw the living symbols of the spirit of the united allied nations. I saw brought to life before my eyes the reasons why the inevitable outcome of the war would be a sweeping victory over the Axis Powers.

A shivering crowd sent its cheers cutting across the bitter winter wind at sight of General Claire Chennault's Flying Tiger crew, the Rangoon Ramblers. These hardy fighters from Asia rode in three Army jeeps at the head of the parade.

Behind them came one brilliantly uniformed detachment after another, each bringing a stab to my heart at the recollection of the things that had been done abroad in the name of modern warfare.

Sailors from the Royal Navy marched with brisk and vigorous steps, and I remembered their heart-breaking fight to hold the Mediterranean Sea. White-skirted Greeks strode by, and I remembered the glorious battle of the Evzones to save their nation from invasion. Then came the Belgians and the Poles, among the

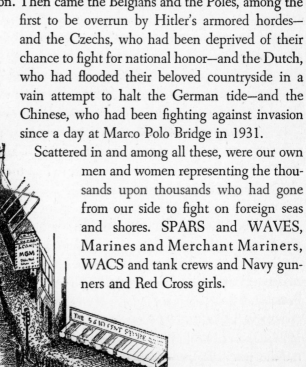

first to be overrun by Hitler's armored hordes—and the Czechs, who had been deprived of their chance to fight for national honor—and the Dutch, who had flooded their beloved countryside in a vain attempt to halt the German tide—and the Chinese, who had been fighting against invasion since a day at Marco Polo Bridge in 1931.

Scattered in and among all these, were our own men and women representing the thousands upon thousands who had gone from our side to fight on foreign seas and shores. SPARS and WAVES, Marines and Merchant Mariners, WACS and tank crews and Navy gunners and Red Cross girls.

It was a parade of United Nations spirit, as keen as the January wind itself and as bright at its heart as the gold leaf dome of the State House that lay temporarily hidden under a wartime coat of gray.

One by one, as the groups from the "Unconquerable" countries reached the front of Jordan Marsh, they came to a solemn halt. Each unit then dedicated a store window specifically arranged to represent the indomitable spirit of its country. I tell you, there have been many proud moments in my 100 years with Jordan Marsh—but nothing to equal the feelings that stirred my heart that day.

We went on with the "Unconquerables" program, long after the parade had passed into memory and the onlookers had hurried away from the cold and windy streets. We went on with the show all through the week, with special events on the fifth floor of the Annex Building—honoring Greece on Monday, Czechoslovakia on Tuesday, Holland on Wednesday, Poland on Thursday, Norway on Friday—and a grand assembly of all the "Unconquerables" on Saturday.

By the time we were through, we had sold war bonds amounting to $18,824,698.

That's what it has been like, living with Jordan Marsh through the nation's greatest wars.

It has been an experience of courage and initiative, of patriotism and strength. It has shown me that as long as there is a New England, there will always be a United States of America ready to defend its national honor and to hold its head high among the governments of the earth.

I learned that fact 90 years ago, when our first flag was run aloft atop our building in Winthrop Square.

Since then, my association with Jordan's has kept that knowledge as bright and as fresh as the very colors of that flag itself.

## Chapter VI

# BY LAND, SEA, AND AIR

Sometimes at night, hours after the shoppers have departed, I like to perch on the corner of the roof of the new building, and look out over the harbor to the open sea, and let my mind travel to the faraway marts of the world.

The best time for this is long after dark, when the city has gone to bed. At that time, tall shadows fall upon the quiet streets outside, and a friendly silence moves across the city blocks below. There is a hush about the place, where so recently thousands of feet were moving back and forth.

I get up and journey from one building of our store to another, and from floor to floor, letting my fancy travel on long journeys to distant markets. The course of my voyage is never the same from night to night, for it depends entirely on the thoughts that are prompted to life by the articles that catch my eye.

The sight of a rich imported rug, for instance, is enough to send me in fancy to the caravan trails of northern Iran. If I stand and listen closely, it seems that I can hear the cries of the merchants and the thin strange wailing music of reeds and flutes in a dusty bazaar many thousands of miles away.

Perhaps this very rug came originally from just such a place. Perhaps two burnoosed tribesmen haggled over the price in terms of dinars and rials. Perhaps then it was slung across the back of a camel, and a few nights later began its long journey to the sea— over the very trails that were known to Alexander the Great, and later to the Roman Legions, and still later to the murderous Mongol horsemen.

And here it is tonight, near the end of its journey, waiting in the shadowy silence of Jordan's and soon to be at rest on the floor of some New England home.

I move away from the rugs and wander off through the darkness, walking about idly until a glimpse of something white catches my eye.

A thin sliver of light is shafting in from the street outside, and falling upon a tall pile of linen goods. These are from Ireland, and as I stand there looking at them I travel in fancy to the land where they were made. I seem to see the green and purple hills of County Galway, and the sun that's going down beyond the bay. I remember the crystal-clear waters of the Corrib river, where salmon by the thousands fight their way upstream to spawn. I remember the beauty of the Golden Vale and the Blackwater Valley. And it warms my heart to think of the pleasure that this linen will bring to some lady of Boston, perhaps tomorrow morning.

Again I walk on through the shadowy store, passing rolls of silk that have journeyed here from China, carved ivory from West Africa, and crystal glassware from Czechoslovakia—passing as well the stores of American products, the steel goods from Pittsburgh, and furniture from Grand Rapids, the textile goods from New England mills, and leather products from Massachu-

setts itself. Each brings its own thoughts to my mind, and makes my fanciful journey a trip of romance and pleasant adventure.

There has always been dramatic color connected with the articles on sale at Jordan's, ever since the company was born 100 years ago.

Back in those days, young Americans were being urged to go West. Gold had been discovered in California. Fortunes were to be made overnight in some cases, and to be lost overnight in others. Great wagon trains were forming for the long and dangerous trek across the continent. And many a New England farmer was abandoning his plow, possibly to be slain at the hands of Indian raiders.

In the midst of this vast turning toward the West, Eben Jordan turned his eyes toward the East—toward the lands that lay beyond the Atlantic. It was not his mission to be part of the surge toward the plains and the mountains. It was his mission to stay in Boston and to help build his company into an organization that would work with New England and build with New England.

Accordingly, he probed the markets of Europe for the goods that could be sold at home—for the best products of skilled craftsmen and generations of artistry. He probed so far toward the east, in fact, that he almost rounded the world and met the New

Englanders who had journeyed west. In time, only the Pacific Ocean lay between them.

These items that he bought—pottery and drapes, jewelry and lace—reached the Jordan Marsh Company at Boston in many ways.

Clipper ships, built and manned by New England hands, skimmed over the blue seas and brought their cargoes home. Railroads were built, and began to tote to Boston the goods that had landed at other harbors. Mule trains came up from the south, and loaded sleighs came down from the north in the wintertime.

As the years went on, the graceful clippers were replaced by steamships. Trucks replaced the wagon trains, and finally the airplane showed the way to the fastest freight transport of all.

These are some of the things I like to remember, walking alone in the store at night. I like to think of the whistling of the wind in the clean white sails of old ships—and the whistling of cargo vessels as they turn from foreign ports and head for home. I like to think of the soft creaking of saddle leather on the horses of old-time salesmen—and the swift roar of four-engined aircraft as they race down faroff runways for their takeoff.

All of these sounds, all of these places, all of these changes, have helped to build the Jordan Marsh Company. And when I'm alone at night, walking about in the shadows of the store, it's pleasant to live with the pictures that come to mind.

I was talking of these things one evening recently, when I'd been invited to dinner by one of my Boston friends.

The family was one of old New England heritage. It had been here for generations, and some of its members had been among the first to start buying from Eben Jordan just after he'd made his first sale of cherry ribbon.

They asked me to their home, and promised me a surprise— though whether it was to come in the form of entertainment or of a new recipe for clam chowder I had no way of knowing.

At any rate, I accepted and went to their house at the appointed time, frankly curious as to what was in store.

We had a pleasant dinner. Then I filled my pipe from my host's special blend of tobacco. We sat there in comfortable silence for a while—my friend, his wife, their son and daughter, their cocker spaniel and myself.

"Well," I said at last, "what's the surprise? Perhaps it's impolite to ask, but I have no control over my own curiosity. What's in store for me now?"

They exchanged smiles. My host lighted a fragrant cigar.

"You're proud of your association with Jordan's, aren't you, my friend?" he asked.

I nodded and blew a remarkable smoke ring.

"Yes," I said, watching the ring curl away. "I am proud of New England. To me, Jordan's is New England in the shape of a great business organization."

"You've talked sometimes about the variety of Jordan's stock," said my host. "You've mentioned the many lands where that stock has been bought—and the many household needs it can fill."

"Every household need," I corrected him. "You could clothe and keep your family through Jordan's, without having to go anywhere else to buy."

"That's the surprise," he said abruptly.

I cast him a puzzled glance. "That's no surprise to me," I

objected. "It's just the very thing that I've been telling you." I went back to my pipe.

He chuckled quietly. "Have you noticed the tie I'm wearing?"

I looked at it casually. "It's a good one," I told him. "Where did you get it?"

"From Jordan's—and Jordan's had it made in New York."

I nodded.

"Have you noticed my watch?" his wife put in. "It came from Jordan's—and originally from Connecticut."

I nodded again. I was beginning to suspect what lay ahead.

"That ash tray, where you just dropped your match, that was made in California," said my host. "The hooked rug under your feet came from the Orient."

"And the stair carpet that leads to this room came from Pennsylvania," said his wife. "All from Jordan's, of course."

"Of course," I agreed. "All from Jordan's. And the cigarette lighter on the table?"

"Chicago," said my friend.

"The Madonna plaque on the wall?"

"Italy."

I caught the spirit of the thing then, and began to mention items at random, ranging from my friend's socks to his wife's sweater.

"The socks from England, the sweater from Scotland," he told me.

"Your porcelain miniatures?"

"From France."

"Your dish towels?"

"Ireland."

"The music box?"

"Switzerland."

As fast as I could toss the questions at them, they answered with the source of everything in the room and everything they wore. There wasn't an item in sight that had not come from Jordan's. Scissors from Germany, slippers from Mexico, a Guatemalan handbag, a piece of French needlepoint—it went on and on until it began to get down right monotonous.

Finally I called a halt. "You must have gone to a lot of work to arrange all this," I told them.

They shook their heads. "As a matter of fact," my host said. "We didn't arrange a thing. It just happened that way. We were sitting here talking about you and the Jordan Marsh Company the other night, and about your birthday celebration, and just for the fun of it we began to check the things in the room to find out how many had come from Jordan's.

"We were amazed at the end of the evening to find that we couldn't name anything that hadn't come from there. Without realizing we were doing it, we had clothed ourselves and furnished our rooms completely with Jordan's products. Of course, a lot of the furnishings were bought in the family years ago. We've simply added to them as time has gone on."

I had a sudden flash. "Aha!" I exclaimed. "Now I've got you. How about that harness on the spaniel?"

My host laughed. "Jordan's again," he told me. "From the Dog Shop."

I shrugged. "You win—I'm happy to say. I've always contended that a man and his family could get all their day-to-day needs filled at our store, but frankly I never expected to see it done so completely."

I stayed late at their home that night, for the conversation clung to the line of Jordan's shipments—a line that I've always found intensely fascinating. They were kind enough to

let me talk about one of my favorite topics, and I rambled along from one story to another.

I told them of the almost astronomical figures that enter our merchandise lists during an average year. For an example, I gave them the figures for 1949, when Jordan's received 219,000 separate shipments.

"How much did that weigh?" asked my friend, expecting to catch me without an answer.

"Exactly 32,504,338 pounds," I told him. "And what's more, it cost the company over $550,000 just to receive the goods that were not pre-paid."

"And how does the stock arrive?" he asked.

"All kinds of ways," I replied. "We get over 10,000,000 pounds a year by rail and over 17,000,000 pounds over the highways by trailer-truck. Also, it arrives by air and parcel post—and I sometimes wonder if we won't be getting it by rocket before we're through.

"And as for the sea lanes, ever since your grandfather skippered his own bark, we've been getting stock by way of the high waves."

He nodded. "You also send items out by the same methods, don't you?"

"Yes," I told him. "We ship by rail and truck and whatever the occasion calls for. And ever since 1947, we've been cooperating with American Airlines in sending 'Friendship Planes' to

the British Isles. Customers buy packages in our Food Shop and address them to friends in England, Scotland and Wales. We load them aboard the planes, and 24 hours later they're on the other side of the Atlantic, and from the letters we've received, they're mighty welcome over there where food is still scarce."

That's the way the talk went, until late into the night. I told them all I knew of the drama of Jordan's merchandise. They were deeply interested, probably remembering that their own forebears had helped to shape this picture by buying from Eben Jordan in the days of the packet ships and the horse-drawn sleighs. I talked so much that occasionally my pipe went out. But my friend was always ready with his private blend, to start me off with a fresh smoke and a fresh string of ideas.

Finally I made my excuses and came home. I should have gone to bed right away, for the bells had long since rung midnight. But I felt I couldn't sleep without one more stroll through the store, from floor to floor and up and down the stairs. Somehow, I wanted to see and touch the good things from distant lands, and to let my mind wander again on imaginary voyages.

It was all there, just as I'd known it so many times before— the shadows slanting down, and the occasional sound from the

streets outside, and the hush that would depart with the morning to make way for the sound of thousands of feet.

And as I moved from one corner to another, I was off again as I'd been so many times in the past—to the harbor at Cherbourg and the beauty of Naples at night—to a dollmaker's shop in Germany, and the home of a weaver in France—to the back room of an English tobacconist, and to the home of an Egyptian brassworker.

It made me feel good, realizing how many people in so many lands were linked to the good people of New England, through the flow of merchandise across the counters of the Jordan Marsh Company.

I slept soundly that night, the way a man sleeps when he's seen a job well done.

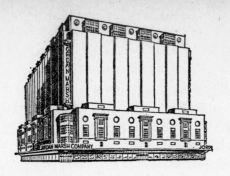

## Chapter VII

# BRICK BY BRICK

My OLD home town of Boston has known many a pleasant surprise in its long and colorful history, but I like to think that the historians of the future will mark a special circle in their books around the date of Thursday, March 27, 1947.

That was the day when commuters on their way to work found on the front pages of their newspapers a story of tremendous importance to the future of New England business. It was President Edward R. Mitton's announcement that the Jordan Marsh Company would build in Boston the greatest department store in the world.

I watched them as they read that story—on the subway cars and in the taxicabs, on the suburban railroad trains and on the back seats of chauffeur-driven automobiles. I hurried around to as many points as I could reach that morning, wherever the crowds stood waiting for transportation, for I wanted to note their first reactions to the news.

I was happy then and I am happy now to report that I found nothing but enthusiastic endorsement. There were innumerable signs of civic pride, born of the thought that the city's biggest department store was moving forward once again, this time into even broader fields than the past had known.

When the rush hour was at its height, and it was impossible for me to cover all the rivers of traffic, I climbed to the highest part of the old Jordan Marsh building and peered down through my spyglass, training it here and there at random upon the moving knots of commuters. Again and again I noticed that their papers were folded to the Jordan story, and I could tell by their faces and gestures that they were discussing the announcement with the utmost of pleasure.

Their reaction was exactly what we had hoped for and, to be frank, what we had expected. The story was one that demonstrated immovable faith in the future of New England, and the readers were quick to sense that fact and to respond in kind.

"A decision has been reached," said President Mitton's statement in part, "which will exert its influence not only upon the future of this business, upon the local community of Boston, and upon the Commonwealth of Massachusetts, but also in fact to a degree upon the whole of New England.

"And so it is that with unbounded confidence in the integrity, stability and future prosperity of this area and community of peoples I am happy to announce our decision to commence a building program."

And toward its end, the statement declared:

"This will be but another expression

of our absolute confidence in the forward-looking spirit of the Boston and New England of today.

"So to the people of this area and community we make this announcement, and as you have given to us of your loyalties, and we have given to you of our services, let us consider this then to be a mutual undertaking so that we may build for Boston and New England 'The One Store of Its Kind in All the World.'"

That's precisely what the public did—it seized upon the project as a mutual undertaking. Probably nothing in the city's entire history of construction has drawn more interested audiences of spectators and sidewalk superintendents than the building of the New Units on Chauncy and up Summer Streets.

Long before they first gathered there, however, they were told just what to expect. The original report convinced them that the Jordan Marsh plans were drawn with an eye to a prosperous and progressive future, and with a loyalty to a rich and historic past. So those plans remain today, and so they will continue through the years of work that lie ahead.

The public was told, for example, that the new Jordan Marsh store would cover a full-block area—an area larger than that of the Harvard Stadium. It would penetrate the depths of the earth to a distance of two stories, and in time it would climb 14 stories high toward the clouds above.

Throughout this mammoth structure there would be the most modern arrangements and conveniences known to the world of construction and design. There would be "talking elevators," with wire recorders announcing each floor and its contents. There would be fleximodule lighting, bringing a daylight glow to the broad aisles and the neat showcases. There would be air conditioning and automatic doorways, off-street ramps for trucks and trailers, miles of steel and aluminum to replace old-fashioned plaster and dust, block-long show windows, protective overhang-

ing marquees, radiant-heated sidewalks that would cleanse themselves of snow and ice—and a hundred other improvements and innovations.

For its link with the past, the plans called for the great new store to be of red brick with white trim, in keeping with the rich dignity of early New England structures. On this point, the designers declared that the store would "stay in the Boston tradition as it continued to evolve—just as would be done if we had continued the tradition of Bulfinch right down to the present." They revealed that the building would present in its appearance "the touch and color and some details reminiscent of the period of 1800."

In other words, brick by brick, this new store of Jordan's would take shape as a warm reminder of New England's heritage and as a herald of the century to come. It would contain in its outward lines and shadings the colonial spirit reflected in the red bricks of Faneuil Hall and of the old State House and of all the other structures where the talented Charles Bulfinch had left his mark. It would offer through its inner conveniences the peak efficiency of the 20th Century.

The public was reminded that this entire project could scarcely be completed in a day or in a year—that Jordan's intended to stay in business while the very walls were taking shape—that the whole program would be undertaken in five steps of one unit each—that in the end, New England would see the five units blended into a beautiful whole—and that within five to seven years, the last of the old stores would have vanished and the last of the new bricks would have been tamped into position.

"As the work continues," the official announcement said, "we feel certain that the complete cooperation of our customers and the general public will keep pace by overlooking certain inconveniences. We ask them to excuse these incidents in the realization that they are unavoidable in the course of such a huge undertaking.

"It is of vital importance to this company and to the project that our confidence in the community reflect itself in an increased dollar volume of business in order that we can continue to grow as we build, and thus at the completion find ourselves with the requisite volume of sales to support the program."

Such was the story that greeted commuters and housewives on that memorable spring morning in 1947.

It was a story that stirred the hearts of the people of New England. They had been asked to regard the project as a "mutual undertaking." They responded by supporting it whole-heartedly from the moment the first workman reported on the job for the start of Unit No. 1.

We had many a good hour together during the building of that first unit—I looking down from a wall as the shovels bit into the earth, the public looking on from the sidewalks and from the sheltered stand that was built for the spectators.

We watched one of our older building sections razed to the ground, and then we saw a great excavation sink deeper and deeper into the rock and dirt between Summer and Avon streets.

When the right depth was reached, we saw the workers build

the rugged foundation of steel and concrete needed to support the levels that would some day loom overhead. We saw them come back to the surface again, and start the tall strong walls of red colonial brick that would bring to modern Boston the color of old New England.

We grew to know each other better than ever, the public and I, as we returned day after day to watch our "mutual undertaking" climb toward completion. We became such warm friends, I remember, that at one time we organized an informal "Observer's Society." The membership button was a picture of myself, and it was given to all the supporters who watched the construction through the special peepholes in the Chauncy Street fence, or who preferred to find a more comfortable observation post and linger a bit longer at the scene.

It was a great day for that society of ours when we cheered the arrival of the biggest piece of steel ever hauled through the streets of Boston. This was a gigantic girder, 72 feet long and weighing 70 tons. It was manufactured in Pennsylvania and shipped east to be placed in position and to support an entire section of the new unit. It occupied three railroad flat cars when it arrived here. Two low-bed trailers had to be linked together to move it from the Southampton

street freight yards to where the trim building was taking shape.

The big day when we laid the cornerstone was on May 21, 1949. That was a day that drew national attention. Greetings poured in from a thousand sources, from the White House at Washington and from the homes of Jordan customers.

I remember Senator Leverett Saltonstall, presiding at the ceremonies. I remember Congressman John W. McCormack, bringing the congratulations of the President. I remember the Mitton speech of dedication, touching upon the features of the unit and declaring:

"This sturdy steel is synonymous of that strength of character for which both New England and Jordan's are famous.

"The red brick is representative of the warmth and friendliness of our New England people and of Jordan's.

"The New England granite is of the ruggedness and basic integrity of both our people and our institution.

"Its touches of modernism suggest the forward-looking principles which have always been the basis of New England progress."

Within the cornerstone that day we placed the tangible reminders of the progress of America, New England, Boston and the Jordan Marsh Company itself. We included a booklet with a brief history of the organization—pictures of the Company's leaders from the time of

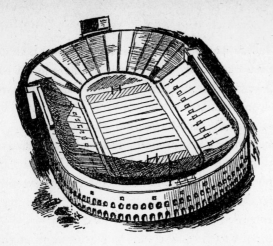

Eben himself—newspapers and currency—signatures of the members of the Half Century Club and the Quarter Century Club —a letter from the President of the United States—copies of speeches—a print of the proposed new building as it would some day look.

Then we sealed the stone, and the first great step was completed.

Since that day, we have moved steadily toward the ultimate goal of completing the entire structure. Brick by brick we have surged ahead—each brick a reminder of New England's proud past, each brick a symbol of her mounting opportunities.

The second building unit was started at the "Turn of our Century" year 1950, and will be completed and dedicated as one of the events during our great Centennial Celebration in 1951.

Its foundations were firmly planted in Boston's historic soil, for it was here at No. 27 Summer Street that Ralph Waldo Emerson was born on May 25, 1803, in the parsonage home of his father.

Here, too, at No. 33 stood the legendary Tory headquarters of Samuel P. Gardner amidst his apple orchard, which is reputed to have been one of the first orchards planted on the North American continent.

I recalled the words of the original building program announcement in which we had stated, "No longer will it be necessary to go to New York or Chicago for the latest there is, because it will be right here in Boston." And now we could demonstrate what we had meant by that.

We had said, "This construction should be executed in such a manner as to be a complement, and at the same time a monument, to the Boston tradition and the New England people who made it possible by their solid support of this business." And we had shown that it would be so.

We had said, "This building will tend to make outmoded by comparison any such commercial establishment which at present stands or is in the process of completion." And we had proved that in the building itself.

We had said, "We will build the one store of its kind in all the world." And we had completed the first step toward that end and started the second.

I remembered the words of an editorial that I had clipped from the Boston Traveler in which it had been written:

"The more we contemplate the vision of the new Jordan Marsh store, with the ultimate in merchandising facilities and techniques—with its architecture that captures New England's past and its wealth of worldly wares which embodies America's present and the world's present and future—the more something that is not physical impresses itself upon our mind.

"It is the courage, the confidence, the serene and unshaken belief this old Boston institution has in Boston. It is the spirit of New England enterprise, a spirit undimmed as decade follows decade.

"The new Jordan Marsh will not spring into being quickly. Its scale will be the grander one. But stage by stage the old will disappear and the new will take its place and the area bounded by Washington, Summer and Avon Streets will become the site of America's finest, most modern and—who knows—largest store.

"This will be new. Yes, and it will be very old indeed. It is in that spirit that Jordan Marsh has served and prospered for nearly a century. Yesterday will join hands with tomorrow in this great enterprise and Boston will remain the commercial heart of New England and one of the great commercial centers of the world."

I slipped away from the crowd then, and went out to stand on the street and to look once more at the red brick exterior of my new home.

I found myself nodding with pleasure. Eben Jordan would have been delighted with the inside, Charles Bulfinch with the outside, and we of the moment were delighted with the whole.

## Chapter VIII

# EACH TO THE OTHER

JUST as the merchant does at the end of the fiscal year, in order to determine his worth, so too there comes a time when every individual should put aside the hustle and bustle of the daily life and quietly take an accounting of his personal assets and his position in the community.

I could think of no better time to take such a reckoning than on my 100th anniversary, and so on that evening I tucked my spyglass under my arm and threaded my way through Boston's older streets and alleys to a little smoke-beamed restaurant of which I knew, and which permitted in its quaint and dimly lighted interior the exact quietude needed for reveries and pensiveness.

Seating myself alone at a table in a far corner, I called for a large pot of coffee, and explained to the waiter—an old friend of mine who was hovering at my elbow—that this was an evening during which I did not wish to be disturbed.

"Do me the favor," I said, "of seeing that I am left completely alone. I intend to sit here and smoke, and attempt to do some

82

very clear thinking. Make certain from time to time that I am supplied with fresh hot coffee, but be a good chap and do not talk to me until I signify that my reverie is at an end."

He smiled understandingly, and after whisking some imaginary crumbs from the linen cloth he slipped away in search of a large pewter pot. He returned with it full of black coffee, and then left me by myself.

I sat there watching the blue tobacco smoke curl from my pipe toward a ship's lantern that hung overhead, and in those climbing curves of smoke I saw the pictures of the years gone by as one by one they drifted into view.

All the good things done for me by my New England friends came tumbling into sight, one after another in rapid sequence.

There were those first days when the sale of a piece of cherry ribbon started us in the retail business. I saw the people coming again and again to buy at our store, showing us by their wants and requests the steps we should take to expand our stock and meet their growing needs.

They were our partners, actually, for it takes two to make a transaction, and in the making there must be satisfaction on both sides if business is to progress.

I saw these good people molding and shaping our futures with their loyalty of patronage, and with their American desire to improve their lives with the necessities and the luxuries of their day.

It was those same customers who taught us that the way to succeed was to heed their advice and to have what they wanted when they wanted it, and at the prices that they wished to pay. After all, in what better way could we serve them?

I saw them helping us through those first hard days of our life, and then nurturing our growth and urging us on to expansion and to progress.

They had been most loyal in their support of us, and they had built that loyalty on a foundation as strong and immovable as the stones of our newest buildings.

Watching the smoke, I saw once again the enthusiasm with which New Englanders had welcomed the Jordan Marsh innovations in the retail world. I saw many an unimaginative merchant shake his head with a dour scowl and predict nothing but trouble and ruin for a company that dared to be progressive—and then I saw the men and women of Boston and Newton and Quincy and a hundred other places recognizing the worth of what Jordan Marsh was trying to do, and following through to success.

There were pictures in the smoke that showed housewives talking to their neighbors, spreading good news about the pleasure of doing business at Jordan's. There were pictures of the neighbors in turn coming in to buy, and themselves going out and suggesting to somebody else to become a Jordan Marsh customer. Every good word spoken of the company was a good turn done by a New Englander, and I smiled with satisfaction as I saw in the smoke the way the welcome news had traveled from home to home.

Time and again, I saw the picture of some New England family deciding against a purchase in some distant city, preferring to wait to get back home and "find it at Jordan Marsh." This meant giving the trade to New England itself, and helping not only the store but the region as well. This was the attitude that brought about the familiar slogan, "You can find it at Jordan's."

I saw young men and women coming from New England's schools and colleges to enter Jordan Marsh and study the retail business, and in turn give the company the benefit of their initiative and intelligence. I saw them coming from New England homes, to work behind the counters and help the company with their energy and good spirits.

Picture after picture showed the people of New England supporting Jordan Marsh—with cash, cooperation and confidence—from the time of its beginning right up to the present hour. And as a result of that support, the pictures showed the company making its steady growth, from a single dry goods counter to the position of one of the largest department stores in the nation.

Then the patterns changed and the smoke hung lazily in the air for a moment or two before it began to take on new shapes.

This time the view was from the other side—the side that showed the many things the Jordan Marsh Company had tried to do in return. It was the public, after all, that had made possible the organization's growth to the rank of fourth largest department store in the United States, and in turn the company had sought in many ways to return the gesture of support and cooperation.

Thus, I saw Jordan Marsh reaffirming its faith in the New England community, leading the way for example in tremendous real estate investments and in stock investments almost without a parallel in the world of merchandising. I thought of how this must have encouraged many a small business man to do likewise, to invest his future in New England hearts and New England hands.

I saw property values mounting, because of the dignity and worth of the Jordan units that were placed in their midst. And I heard the wheels of production move at a faster tempo, as business owners followed the Jordan example and expanded their stock.

I considered the importance of Jordan Marsh participation in

all the community movements—the
Red Cross and the U. S. Savings
Bond drives, the Community Fund
and the American Cancer Fund.
There was no way, I knew, of
measuring the value of the Jordan
Marsh influence on such drives, for
values of that sort are interwoven
with the general public welfare and
make themselves known only in the
form of better community living
conditions.

I looked again, and I saw a pic-
ture of a tremendous crowd of people—a crowd bigger than many
a metropolitan city—500,000 persons in all. I recognized there the
number of persons holding credit accounts today at Jordan's, benefiting by that credit system which the company itself had introduced to the business world.

For several moments, I tried to estimate how many people in
the end might be affected by these credit accounts, but the
problem was too vast. By actual record, I knew, Jordan's held
a top position among the great stores of the world in the matter
of credit and charge accounts. It seemed safe to estimate that
2,000,000 people might benefit each month by this system—a
staggering figure, and yet a figure that was based wholly upon
fact and logic.

Then a host of scenes came swirling through the smoke,
showing in one way after another how the Jordan Marsh Company had tried to repay the people of New England for their
loyalty and support through the years.

I saw the organization in its strong promotion of New England culture—art, literature, music and all. I recalled the annual

exhibition of paintings by contemporary New England artists, held regularly for more than 20 years. Here I saw the people of Boston and the surrounding countryside entering the Jordan Marsh galleries, to study the works of some 250 painters. I saw them drinking their tea and admiring the good landscapes and marines and portraits. I saw them voting for their favorites, and applauding the winners of the Richard Mitton memorial awards.

"Surely this is good," I said to myself. "Good, that a company like Jordan's can find time to encourage real talent and bring pleasure to the thousands who see these paintings."

I saw prominent authors and stars of the theater being entertained at Jordan's, and meeting the men and women who had known the store as a friend from childhood.

And as I thought of childhood, I remembered the touching tributes that are Jordan's each year at Christmas time. This store was one of the first in the land to reflect the true meaning of Christmas—the first to place its own interests aside and to present in its window displays the ever-loved scenes of the Nativity. And I smiled a bit, thinking of the joy and enthusiasm of the youngsters upon meeting Santa Claus in the Jordan "Toyland" department once each year—of the Christmas Caravan entertainment unit that goes out to spread the Yuletide spirit among hospitals and institutions, carrying gifts and happiness to those less fortunate of our children.

The longer I sat there, sipping my hot coffee and smoking my pipe, the more I realized how little I knew about the far-spread influence of Jordan's upon the life of New

England. Even I, with all my years of close association, had not realized the vast breadth of the circle where the name of Jordan Marsh brought a pleasant reaction, and helped toward better living. For example, I thought of the fact that Jordan's does more newspaper advertising than any similar organization in the world —and I tried to build from there a vision of how this affected the lives of millions of people—of writers and copy-readers and news dealers—of their families and friends—of artists and messenger boys—of clerks in banks, where these people deposited their savings—of subscribers in their homes, studying the advertisements—and of the families and friends of all of these.

It was a hopeless project, trying to grasp that scene, for it overlapped into economics and marriage and every field imaginable.

It led, for instance, to the Jordan Marsh television and radio programs, and there I ran into the same problem—a problem of constantly widening influence and constantly multiplying numbers. And the same thing held true when I thought of seamen who man the ships that bring foreign products to Jordan's home port—and railroad workers on the freights that bring American products across the land—and automobile workers who build the trucks that deliver Jordan's goods—and I realized that the field, in short, was well nigh boundless.

I understood suddenly and with a start of surprise that whatever a New Englander's occupation or his hobby, I could easily show a link to the influence of Jordan Marsh.

I thought too of the specialty programs, the fashion shows, the clubs for youngsters. One by one, I began to check them in my mind.

There was the Connie Cut-up Club, composed of some 3600 young girls from seven to 13 years old, all eager to join the annual contest to find the typical "pigtailer" of the year. There was the

Marsha Jordan Club, with 5000 'teen-age girls choosing the princess of their group to be named "Marsha Jordan" once each year.

There was the annual college style show, with girls from the campuses of New England modeling up-to-the-minute wardrobes. There was the "Women Who Work" program, with lectures on styles and charm for the women of 18 Boston organizations—and the annual lecture clinic for teachers—and the yearly fashion show for the Guild of the Infant Saviour.

Then I thought for a moment of the 7000 fellow workers who keep the company operating, and I saw in the smoke a picture of them taking their pay envelopes into 7000 homes, supporting the lives of nearly 30,000 persons—who in turn influence the lives of thousands of other persons.

It occurred to me suddenly that when I had thought of the 2,000,000 persons affected by the Jordan Marsh credit accounts, I actually had been dealing in conservative figures. Taken as a whole, the scope of Jordan influence was beyond comprehension —beyond the grasp of my mathematical talents.

And occupying an important place in the whole pattern were the names of many individuals and companies who helped not only in the actual building of Jordan structures and the selling of merchandise, but even in such things as the publication of this very book as well. I decided then and there to list them together at the close of this narrative, under the heading of "Centennial Associates."

With that, I rapped my pipe on the edge of an ash tray and prepared to leave. The smoke hung lazily in the air for a moment and then faded away. Surely, I thought—surely New England owes it to itself to keep such an organization as this in good and prosperous health. Surely Jordan's owes it to New England to offer the best of everything and the finest in modern merchandising methods.

In short, I decided, the best of all combinations is the one that now exists—Jordan's and New England, each for the other.

I arose and reached for my spyglass, to start the late walk home. My friend the waiter came quickly to the table to help me with my jacket and to bid me good night.

"You have been very quiet," he observed.

"I have been balancing my books," I replied, picking up my tobacco pouch.

"I saw no books," he remarked.

"No?—But I saw them very clearly," I told him. "I have been examining my assets—considering my position in the scheme of things.

"I find I am on good relations with my very close friend and excellent business partner, the New England community.

"And believe me, my friend, I intend to keep it that way."

With that, I bade him good night.

He was looking after me with a smile of agreement as I went whistling out the doorway and into the darkened street.

## Chapter IX

# EYES TO THE FUTURE

As OLD Eben Jordan used to say, "There's a time for looking backward and a time for looking forward." As for me, there's never been a time for looking forward such as this—the year of my 100th birthday.

For one thing, I like to stroll around the corners of Washington and Summer and Chauncy Streets, standing sometimes with my hands behind my back and my pipe in my mouth, looking up at the buildings of the Jordan Marsh Company. I like to look forward to the day when my new home will be finished—to squint my eyes and to see in fancy the graceful lines and colors that the new units will add to the Boston scene.

I like to visit the homes of my friends, and to talk with them about the golden future of Boston and New England—the future we are entering together, now that we have passed the middle of this century.

And I like to welcome these same friends to my own home, for conversations that probe into the years ahead and yet that slip from time to time into the good things of the years gone by.

Invariably, these days, in my home or theirs, my friends bring up the subject of my birthday. Recently they've been suggesting that they'd like to give me a party, decorated with a mountainous cake and 100 candles. The candles, they point out, would represent not only my years among them but also the warmth of mutual interest in which the New England public and the Jordan Marsh Company have worked together since the day when Eben Jordan first stepped behind a counter.

I always shake my head at such ideas, and plead with them not to plan any such thing. I argue that there is far more reason for gratitude on my side than on theirs, and that if I tried to return their gesture I'd be carrying lighted candles to thousands upon thousands of homes and probably find myself classified as a walking fire menace!

I was deeply touched, when this birthday cake proposal was brought to my very door. It was voiced by a group that came to my room at night, interrupting me as I was examining the ships in Boston harbor through my spyglass. I listened, and thanked them, but I shook my head.

"I've almost completed my book," I told them. "That takes care of all the memories and the looking-backward. It tells of the things that will always stay deep in my heart. Now it is time for the looking-forward."

They understood, just as the people of New England always have understood the sincerity behind the Jordan Marsh motives. And so they left me alone with my spyglass, and after a while I went from my room, down upon the streets and walked to the waterfront.

I went out to the end of a deserted wharf, and sat there on a tar-stained piling, ignoring the protests of the seagulls that had been occupying the spot. I watched the ships as they moved slowly in from the sea, their lights blinking across the channel waters. From time to time a plane droned overhead, slanting down in a long glide toward the airport across the harbor. The smell of clean fresh salt air came in on the breeze and left me completely relaxed.

I tried to look ahead to the years that were coming, and to picture the part of Jordan Marsh in the drama of tomorrow. The sight of the ships, and the lights on the tidal water, brought thoughts of the bright future of Boston, with cargoes coming in from all corners of the world and with passengers arriving from distant lands. The drone of the planes reminded me of the great dreams for Boston's airport, with Europe only a few hours away in one direction and the vast spread of America only a few hours away in the other.

From each of these visions, I pictured men and women coming to New England with fresh ideas for progress and with new contracts for gigantic steps in industry. And I saw New Englanders themselves being called away as they had been called for generations, to plant the seeds of stability and energy in distant fields— but always to return at the end of their task and to take up their lives among us once again.

I saw Jordan's secure in its role as the greatest store in our midst, and I saw the families of tomorrow working and living in harmony with the organization just as did the families of yesterday and of 100 years ago.

As I sat there, feeling the salt breeze against my face, I listened to the quiet sounds of the city behind me. I thought of how different it would be in the morning, with the tread of thousands of feet, the symphony of automobile engines, the rushing of subway cars and the smooth grind of railroad wheels.

That would be the sound of New Eng-

land business on the move, the heartbeat of a strong industrial giant. It would be the sound of motion and of building—of the vast churning and singing that goes with progress—of the machines in many factories, producing goods that soon would be sold in Jordan's—creating new products from great new inventions—turning out a host of 20th century articles, each in turn to become one more link between the Jordan Marsh Company and its New England friends.

But now it was night, and it was quiet. And my thoughts came back to the moment at hand.

I looked out across the harbor toward the east, and I thought to myself how fitting it is that New England each day catches the first rays of the rising sun as it travels from the Old World to the New. It was truly appropriate, I told myself, for the newborn sun is always a symbol of hope and promise and fresh opportunities—and surely nowhere on earth do these elements mean more to mankind than within the historic borders of New England.

Ours is a rich heritage. Together, we have fought for its values and its truths in times of war and peace. We have toiled for them in times of hardship. We have drawn upon them and cherished them in times of prosperity. We shall adhere to them through all the coming years.

That is the way it always has been with the good people of New England and with the Jordan Marsh Company. That is the way it was 100 years ago, when a little girl bought a piece of cherry ribbon and thereby started Jordan Marsh on its long and pleasant journey to this day. And that is the way it will remain, whatever the coming years may hold.

That hope was warm in my mind, as I rapped my pipe on the edge of the piling and knocked out the old ashes to make room for the new. I tucked my spyglass under my arm, looking at it affectionately a moment as at an old and trusted companion.

Then I rose to my feet and prepared to go home, to start a new century of comradeship with my best and most loyal of friends.

The sound of my footsteps mingled with the quiet sounds of the city about me, and as I walked along my way, I looked up at the stars and spoke the words that were closest to my heart:

"God willing, the coming years will keep us together—a pleasant life for the good of all."

With that thought, I enter with confidence upon my second century.

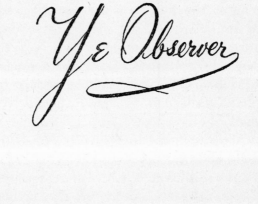

*Ye Observer*

*"As with our fathers,
so God be with us"*

RALPH WALDO EMERSON

# CENTURY CLUB MEMBER

Ye Observer

# HALF CENTURY CLUB MEMBERS

I record herewith the names of my Fellow Workers who have shown their devotion to this organization for fifty years or more.

Evelyn Anderson
Rosa C. Beagin
* Allan Bertram
* Andrew L. Better
* Ephraim J. Boleman
* Annie L. Brine
Mary A. Bryans
* Dennis J. Cahan
* Mary A. Callahan
* William C. Clark
* Frank Coleman
* Margaret A. Connelly
* Marie A. Connelly
John F. Cooney
* William J. Corbett
* Mary A. Coughlin
* Elizabeth M. Courtney
John J. Cronin
* Catherine M. Crowley
John E. Crowley
Elizabeth L. Daley
James P. Devine
M. Grace Devine
Joseph P. Devlin
Mary C. Dunlevy
Helen M. Egan
* James J. Evans

Abbie S. Fay
* Nellie M. Feeley
Delle F. Feely
Nellie T. Feeney
Mary A. Fife
* Mary E. Flatley
* Anna M. Fogel
Peter H. Forest
* Thomas F. Garrity
* Thomas F. Giblin
Cecilia A. Glavey
* Nathaniel W. Goodwin
* James Grainger
Silas Guggenheim
* Alice V. Hardy
Mary L. Hogan
Mary L. Hughes
Thomas F. Hughes
* Nellie A. Kane
* Emmett J. Kelley
* Fred C. Kemball
* John W. Kenney
Elizabeth F. Lalley
* William F. Larrabee
Anna V. Leary
Elizabeth Lennon
Thomas J. Lonergan

* Annie G. Lyons
  Valentine E. MacFaden
  Katherine A. Maddock
  Mary A. Magee
* Mary A. Maney
  Mary M. McCarthy
  William J. McCarthy
  Anna F. McCourt
  Catherine G. McDevitt
  Julia A. McDevitt
* Mary A. McDonough
* Katherine M. McGlashing
* Mary A. McLaughlin
  Sadie G. McNulty
* George W. Mitton
  Mary F. Morris
  Annie G. Murphy
  Margaret L. Murphy
* Alice F. Nagle
* Mary T. Neary
* Alice M. Nolan
  E. Florence Nolan

  Frank W. O'Brien
* Otho T. O'Leary
  Jennie M. Patten
  Edward J. Pendergast
  Mary T. Prendergast
  Mary E. Quigley
  Edward Reinhardt
* James Rogers
* Elizabeth A. Ronayne
* Julia E. Rowell
* Frederick W. Russell
* Annie E. Ryan
* William J. Ryan
  Alfred H. Schaltenbrand
  Francis Small
  William H. Stevens
  Katherine J. Sutton
  Anna F. Tobin
  Joseph S. Vogel
* Walter F. Watters
* George F. Weeks
* Norman K. Whitcher

  * Deceased

98

# QUARTER CENTURY CLUB MEMBERS

I record herewith the names of my Fellow Workers who have shown their devotion to this organization for twenty-five years or more.

Albert H. Adams
Ella L. Alcott
Leah F. Alessi
John W. Allen
* Neil M. Allen
Clarence E. Anderson
Elliott C. Anderson
* John A. Anderson
* Ida M. Andrews
Clara M. Annis
Charles W. Appleton
Ada Arnold
Ellen D. Arris
* Francis N. Atherton
* E. P. Atkinson
* Lillian L. Averill
Mary B. Bagley
Catherine Baker
Peter G. Bales
John J. Ballantine
John Ballas
* Belle Balsom
* Catherine Barrett
Eleanor R. Barrett
Helen M. Barry

* Michael Barry
* Patrick D. Barry
Rebecca F. Bartley
* Priscilla Bateman
Mark J. Bates
* Martin Batson
* Thomas Batts
* George A. Bean
* Hortense Beauvais
Minnie M. Beckwith
* Katherine Beirne
* Florence Benn
Edith M. Benson
Alma Benthall
Carl Bergstrom
H. A. Bernau
* Charles H. Berry
Harry S. Beville
Joseph A. Black
Minnie E. Blackden
* George I. Blair
Margaret A. Blanchard
Katherine A. Bonner
Sue T. Bonner
* Daniel Bostwick

William M. Bowler
John J. Boyle
* A. P. Bradford
* C. J. Brady
Thomas P. Brady
Joseph H. L. Brehm
Morris C. Brennan
* Lewis E. Brier
Alice G. Brine
Alice M. Brine
Bonnie H. Brine
* Henry A. Broman
Annie Brown
Margaret A. Brown
William Browne
Marion L. Bruker
Margaret F. Buckley
Thomas J. Buckley
* Carrie A. Bugbee
Jules Bulkowski
Eva M. Bullard
Richard H. Bullard
* Ruth Bullard
Vincent W. Bullard
Theodore A. Burbank
* Elizabeth H. Burke
Gertrude M. Burke
Helen G. Burke
* Joseph Burke
Mae E. Burke
Mary Burke
Ruth M. Burke
Emma Burnett
* Arthur Burwell
Mary L. Butler
Paul W. Butman
Michael J. Buttimer
Margaret M. Buttomer
* W. W. Buxton
Claire M. Byrne
Margaret E. Byrnes
Augusto S. Cabral
Joseph Cabral
Harry F. Cade
Olga E. Cademartori
John B. Cadigan
Mary F. Cahill
Florence E. L. Callahan

Mary E. Callahan
Mary T. Callahan
* Michael J. Callanan
John J. Calnan
Lena O. Cambridge
* James Campbell
Ella Capuana
Helen J. Carbone
Martha M. Card
Warren E. Carey
William J. Carrol
Clara A. Carroll
* Elizabeth I. Carroll
Jane A. Carroll
* Mary E. Carter
Frederick G. Carver
Ethel C. Cates
Margaret Cavanaugh
Mary A. Cavanaugh
* Mary V. Cavanaugh
Ronald D. Cave
Annie M. Chaloux
* James Chambers
Mildred J. Chambers
* Roger Chambers
* Charles L. Chase
Marie O. Cheek
Hilda W. Cheney
Maud M. Chinn
Madeline F. Christie
Anthony M. Cianci
* Mary F. Claffey
Mary A. Clancy
Thelma D. Clapp
* William A. Clark
Isabel Clasby
Katherine E. Cleveland
Margaret E. Clough
* Frank Coburn
Lena Cohen
Randolph T. Colby
Herbert N. Colcord
* Maud Coldrick
* Elizabeth T. Coleman
Helena J. Coleman
J. Gertrude Coleman
Mary E. Collette
Alice L. Collins

* Dennis F. Collins
* Patrick F. Collins
* M. J. Commins
* Peter J. Conboy
Anthony P. Concannon
Margaret L. Conley
* Martin Conlon
* James Conner
Josephine M. Conners
Jeremiah F. Connor
* John H. Connorton
* Hannah F. Conroy
* Katherine E. Conroy
H. C. Conway
Mary S. Conway
* F. W. Coombs
Mary Cooney
Daniel J. Corbett
Matthew Corbett
Randall J. Corbett
Mary G. Corcoran
* James W. Corliss
* Rebecca A. Corthell
Arthur J. Coté
Anna A. Coughlan
Helen C. Coughlin
* Josephine M. Coughlin
Henry P. Coyne
James P. Coyne
Mabel N. J. Craig
* Myra Craig
Joseph S. Craigue
David Crammond
* Egbert A. Crawford
Chester H. Crichett
Anna E. Cronin
Mary M. Cronin
Timothy Crowe
* Catherine T. Crowley
David J. Crowley
Katherine M. Crowley
Mary J. Crowley
Robert L. Crowley
Timothy E. Crowley
Gladys L. Cullity
Sarah C. Cunniff
* Grace G. Cunningham
Mary T. Cunningham

Nora F. Cunningham
Augusta Rita Curley
Jane J. Curran
Margaret V. Curran
Agnes V. Cusick
* Benjamin J. Cutliffe
* Leonard J. Dacey
Catherine Daley
* Margaret A. Daley
Edward S. Daly
Joseph M. Daly
Ellen Darcey
* Edward Darling
* A. D. Davenport
Alice M. Davis
Caroline E. Davison
Alice E. Day
John T. Day
* William Deagan
* John Dealey
* Hannah Decker
Margaret A. DeCourcy
Raymond D. DeCourcey
Marie Alvina DeGrace
* Margaret M. Delaney
John A. DeLuca
Nora A. Dempsey
Lilian A. Dermody
* Ulina Desjardines
* Margaret H. Devine
Julia J. Dilworth
Elizabeth M. Dineen
* William J. Dingivan
Nicholas A. DiSalvo
Eva Dobkin
Belle Doherty
James J. Doherty
Madeline B. Doherty
* Margaret L. Doherty
Margaret M. Doherty
* Mary F. Doherty
Bernard J. Donaher
Margaret F. Donahue
* Kate Donegan
Mary F. Donnelly
Elizabeth M. Donohue
* Catherine E. Donovan
* Nellie Dorris

* Fannie M. Dowling
Charles R. Doyle
Marion Doyle
* Helen B. Drillio
* Elizabeth Drinkall
* Annie Drinkwater
Kathryn F. Driscoll
Mary E. Driscoll
* C. A. Duffey
* Sarah Duffy
* M. J. Dugan
Harry S. Duley
* J. A. Duncan
* Catherine Dunn
* Mary Durbin
Leslie Durkee
Michael E. Dwyer
Nellie A. Dwyer
Daniel F. Eagan
James J. Earley
Maud M. Eddy
Marshall Edwards
Richard H. Edwards, Jr.
Eugene O. Egan
Mabel Egan
* Margaret Egan
Mary Egan
* Mary A. Emerson
Adolph Erlich
* Frederick M. Ethridge
* Alonzo J. Everett
William A. Everett
James H. Fairclough, Jr.
* Mary Fallon
Mary C. Fallon
* Winifred F. Fallon
Marie A. Falvey
Anna L. Farley
* Charles H. Farley
Winifred E. Farley
Tilbury E. Farrenden
* Mary E. Fay
* George E. Fennell
Sadie E. Field
John V. Finn
* Michael A. Finn
William J. Finn
* Ella G. Finnegan

* Helen Finnerty
A. E. Finney
Byron E. Finney
Helena V. Fisher
* W. S. Fisher
* Charles Fitzgerald
* Daniel J. Fitzgerald
* John T. Fitzgerald
* Josephine Fitzgerald
Lillian M. Fitzgerald
* Margaret Fitzgerald
* Margaret Fitzgerald
* Mary Fitzgerald
Mary E. Fitzgerald
Katherine E. Fitzmaurice
Ellen J. Fitzpatrick
* F. A. Flagg
Emily G. Flaherty
Ella R. Flavelle
Lillian C. Flavelle
* Mary A. Fogarty
Julia R. Foley
Katherine J. Foley
* Margaret A. Foley
Mary V. Foley
Frank V. Fonseca
James F. Fonseca
Joseph H. Forbush
* Daniel J. Ford
Lucy A. P. Fraize
Arthur Frank
Mollie L. Fraytus
* Annie E. French
Andrew Frieberg
* Cassie J. Fuller
Augustus J. Furdon
Arthur Gaffney
Gertrude C. Gahagan
Helen Gallagher
* Nellie Gallivan
* Carrie Gammon
Mary E. Gangi
Arthur E. Garrity
Anna C. Garvey
Esther Gaston
Catherine Gately
Francis W. Gately
Martin J. Gately

* Henry B. Gates
Catherine A. Gavin
Helen Gavin
* Mary Gay
Dennis Geaney
* Alice Geary
* James J. Geegan
Martha L. Geer
Eugene M. Getchell
Bruce S. Gilchrist
Hugh D. Gillis
* Margaret Glancy
* James Glennon
Ernest C. Glover
* Frank M. Glynn
Alexander Goldsmith
Margaret Gordon
Marion L. Gordon
James V. Gorman
Katherine E. Gorman
Catherine E. Gormley
Arnold E. Grade
Georgianna F. Grady
* Patrick Grady
* Charles P. Graham
Henry J. Grainger
* Meylert Granger
Russell C. Grant
Alexander R. Gray
Daniel T. Green, Jr.
* Malcolm Green
Mary E. Green
Anna F. Greene
* D. W. Grenham
Daniel E. Griffin
Mary A. Griffin
Ruth E. Griffin
* George H. Guest
Mary J. Gunning
James W. Hagan
* Peter Haglund
Alma C. Hale
Roy Hall
Nan Hallett
* Margaret Hallion
* Nettie Hamelburg
* Mary E. Hamilton
* Susan Hamilton

Loring W. Hamm
* Elizabeth B. Hanly
Ralph J. Hansen
Anna M. Harding
Frances K. Harding
* Martha Hardy
Mildred C. Harmon
* George H. Harney
* Irene S. Harney
Florence Harrington
* Teana V. Harrington
* Nellie Hartnett
Elizabeth Hartrey
* Lillian M. Hatchard
Albert C. Hauck
W. A. Hawkins
Samuel J. Haworth
Anna S. Hayes
* Catherine Hayes
Mary C. Hayes
* Arthur J. Hea
* Alice Healey
Daniel W. Healey
Nora E. Healey
* Frances Hearn
* Minnie L. Hearn
Sadie A. Hedstrom
* Jennie V. Herlihy
Laurinda M. Herlihy
* Teresa A. Heroux
Nellie V. Hicks
Katherine F. Higgins
* Margaret E. Higgins
Alice M. Hill
* Charles I. Hill
* Josephine M. Hill
Ann L. Hogan
* Bridget Hogan
Mollie Hogan
Elizabeth R. Holland
* Madeline F. Honold
* Mary Hopkins
* George H. Horsman
* Margaret Hourihan
* Elizabeth Howe
Joseph E. Howe
* Frank H. Howes
* Harry M. Howes

* Joseph F. Howley
Sherwin E. Hubbard
Lillian F. Huguenard
Harry H. Hull
* Blanche Hunt
Gertrude E. Huntoon
Guy D. Hupper
* Charles H. Hurd
* Charles J. Hurley
Mary V. Hurley
Nan H. Hurley
Katherine T. Hutchinson
Elizabeth Inglis
* Augustus P. Ives
Annie Jacobson
Isadore Jacobson
* Margaret Jason
Philip W. Jefferson
Anna Johnson
Mary A. Johnson
Thelma M. Johnson
* W. V. Jonah
* Delia Jones
* Susan B. Jones
* Charles F. Jordan
Mary T. Joyce
* Sarah F. Joyce
Tyna M. Kaddy
Jennie A. Kadlec
Manuel Kashkashian
Susie L. Keaney
Edna M. Keefe
Mary C. Keefe
* Susan Keefe
Catherine Keenan
Margaret Keevey
Thomas Keiran
Elizabeth M. F. Kelleher
Alice G. Kelley
* James J. Kelley
John T. Kelley
Mary A. Kelley
Mary J. Kelley
* Thomas H. Kelley
Catherine C. Kelly
* John A. Kelly
Julia A. Kelly
Mary E. Kelly

Mary J. Kelly
Cleopha Kempton
* Caroline Kennedy
George M. Kennedy
* James J. Kenney
Mary A. Kenney
Mary E. Kenney
James A. Keough
Joseph T. Kiley
Walter J. Kiley
Agnes Killea
James J. Killion
* Margaret A. Kilmartin
* Catherine J. Kilroy
* William King
* Elizabeth Kneeland
Herbert L. Kruger
John L. Kruger
Ina D. Laflin
* Anna R. Lally
Annie M. Lamb
Ethel J. Lamb
* John Lamb
Mabelle J. Lane
Stephen Lane
Bernice M. Lanigan
Marie E. Lanigan
* William A. Larkin
Pontus E. Larson
Mary Lavender
* Joseph R. Lawson
* Sara Leahy
Frances T. Leary
Dorothy C. Leavitt
Elizabeth A. LeDiouris
Mary A. Lee
* Joseph M. Legarde
Leah G. Legge
John A. Lehan
Blanche C. Leighton
* George H. Leighton
Catherine Lennon
* Ambrose T. Leslie
* Charles Leslie
Mary M. Lester
Rosana M. Leveille
Louis Levine
Emma F. Libby

Helen E. Linnane
Sanford Litwin
* T. F. Lockney
* Lula E. Lombard
* Walter N. London
* William J. Long
Edward E. Lord
* John Lord
* E. A. Loud
Helen F. Lund
* Annie F. Lynch
* Frank M. Lynch
* Jeremiah Lynch
Rosalie M. Lynch
Annie F. Lyons
* Annie G. Lyons
Sarah Lyons
Theresa M. Macauley
* Ellen MacDonald
Ethel A. MacDonald
Helen J. MacDonald
* James J. MacDonald
Murray H. MacDonald
Manuel B. Macedo
* Anna E. Mack
* Mary Mackell
Lillian MacKenzie
Malcolm Macleod
John R. MacMillan
* Nellie MacNeill
Sarah MacWilliams
Alice E. Madden
* Josephine Madden
* Florence Magee
* Thomas Magee
Helen W. Magoon
Agnes M. Maguire
Leo Maguire
Margaret Mahan
* Elizabeth Mahoney
Margaret A. Mahoney
Catherine E. Malloy
H. Wallace Maloney
Lorin F. Maloney
Mary Maloney
Mary A. Maloney
Thomas Maloney
* George J. Manning

* Ada Marks
Mark Marks
Albert E. Marley
Paul Marsh
Anna R. Martin
Katherine G. Martin
Margaret Martin
Marion G. Martis
Carl H. Mattson
Annie Maughan
Catherine C. Maybay
* C. J. Mayo
Adeline C. McAvinue
Catherine E. McCabe
Alice V. McCafferty
* James McCalden
Anna E. McCarthy
Catherine McCarthy
Geraldine M. McCarthy
Lillian M. McCarthy
Mary A. McCarthy
* Sarah McCarthy
* James M. McCathie
Margaret E. McClafferty
Matilda C. McClellan
Mary L. McCormack
Mary E. McCrea
Katherine R. McDevitt
* Mary E. McDevitt
* Annie McDonald
Elizabeth M. McDonald
James McDonald
* Joseph P. McDonald
Margaret McDonald
Mary E. McDonald
Mildred A. McDonald
Edward A. McElroy
* John A. McGaffigan
Martin J. McGagh
William N. A. McGillivary
James J. McGrath
* John J. McGraw
Margaret R. McIntosh
Alice F. McKinnon
* Archie McKittrick
Annie McLaughlin
Catherine L. McLaughlin
* John McLaughlin

* John J. McLaughlin
* Mary McLaughlin
  Mary A. Mclean
* Charles F. McMahon
  Margaret A. McMahon
  Dorothy A. McManus
  Mary L. McManus
  Agatha C. McMullen
* Edward McNamara
  Joseph B. McNamee
* Thomas McNanmon
  John J. McTiernan
  Anthony Meadows
  Marion F. Mee
  Sarah Melhado
  John P. Menton
  Nellie V. Menton
* Charles M. Merchant
* E. B. Merrow
  Rose Mikaelian
  Helen V. Mikulec
  Gladys V. Miller
  Katherine L. Miller
  Lawrence E. Miller
* Agnes Minihan
  Alfred J. Mitchell
  Florence M. Mitchell
  George F. Mitchell
* Thomas J. Mitchell
  Edward R. Mitton
* Richard Mitton
  Robert Mitton
  Richard L. Moberg
  Martin Molloy
* Ethel F. Mongeau
  Lillian J. Montgomery
* Julia Mooney
  Sadie L. Mooney
  Augustine J. Moran
  Eleanor E. Moran
  Margaret Morgan
  Irene E. Morris
  Elizabeth Morson
  Helen J. Morton
* Alice Mulcahy
* Annie Mulcahy
  Michael J. Mulcahy
* Alice C. Mullen

  Grace H. Munroe
  Margaret I. Munroe
* Isaac Murdock
  Helen M. Murnane
  Agnes A. Murphy
  Agnes L. Murphy
  Anna E. Murphy
  Daniel J. Murphy
* Dennis Murphy
  Ellen C. Murphy
  Frederick G. Murphy
* J. F. Murphy
  Josephine E. Murphy
* Julia Murphy
* M. J. Murphy
  Mary E. Murphy
* Mattie J. Murphy
  Nellie J. Murphy
  Nora E. Murphy
  Philip Murphy
* Rosana I. Murphy
  Sadie Murphy
  Theresa M. Murphy
  William F. Murphy
* John Murray
  James F. Navin
  Anna P. Neal
  Agnes G. Neary
* Ida Neary
* Peter J. Nephin
  Florence J. Neville
  Helen Newell
  Earle M. Newton
  Evelyn Newton
  Bertha M. Noble
  Florence L. Noel
* Kate Nolan
  Mary E. Nolan
  Rose M. Nolan
  A. Josephine Norris
  Bertha L. Norris
* Alice M. Nugent
* James J. Nyhan
  Laura Oatis
  Catherine G. O'Brien
  Edith E. O'Brien
* Helen O'Brien
  Helen V. O'Brien

Julia E. O'Brien
Martha A. O'Brien
Mary O'Brien
Mary E. O'Brien
Elizabeth O'Connell
Augustine M. O'Connor
Helen V. O'Connor
Margaret T. O'Connor
Roy F. O'Connor
Anna V. O'Donnell
* William F. O'Donnell
Francis W. O'Hara
* J. H. O'Hara
* John B. O'Kane
Lillian G. O'Keefe
Patrick J. O'Leary
Ella S. Olive
* Kathryn F. O'Neil
* Thomas H. O'Neil
George R. Orr
Margaret O'Toole
* Hugh Owens
Philip J. Owens
Joseph Pacheco
* Lewis Palmer
Henry E. Paré
* L. N. Parker
Madeline Parsons
* George F. Patridge
Clarence A. Peaslee
Bertha A. Pendergast
Grace M. Pendleton
* William Penman
Henrietta Pepler
Anthony H. Perry
* Nellie Peters
Marguerite G. Petersen
Edgar H. Phillips
* F. G. Pickering
* E. L. Pierce
Frederick A. Pierce
* Rae R. Pierce
Rita Pilgrim
* E. A. Pitman
Edward M. Pleadwell
* Christine Powers
* Marion J. Pullen
* Walter Purrington

Margaret E. Quinlan
Anna Quinn
* Mary A. Quinn
Mary V. Quinn
Sarah M. Quinn
Alice M. Ray
Kathryn T. Reddy
Eva C. Redhouse
* Cyrus A. Reed
John T. Reed
* Katherine Reed
* Philomena Reed
* Theodore M. Reed
Edith G. Reeves
* Agnes L. Regan
Elsie C. Regan
R. C. H. Reid
* William J. Relph
* Susette Willey Reneger
* Helen A. Reynolds
Katherine Reynolds
* Louise Reynolds
Anna M. Rezendes
James Rezendes
Virginio Rezendes
* Albert Richards
Florence Richmond
Henry W. Ridings
Ambrose I. Riley
John D. Riley
* Mary E. Riley
Minnie E. Riley
* J. H. Ringot
Evelyn G. Robbins
* John H. Robertson
Carroll L. Robinson
Clement L. Robinson
* Lawson Robinson
* S. L. T. Robinson
Catherine M. Roche
James J. Rockett
James J. Rooney
* William Ross
Elizabeth L. Rourke
* Gertrude Russell
* Albert B. Ryan
Joseph J. Ryan
Leo J. Ryan

* Michael Ryan
Nellie M. Ryan
* Patrick Ryan
* Sarah Ryan
* George P. Ryley
Benjamin F. Samson, Jr.
Bessie Sandler
Henrietta M. Sargent
* George W. Saul
* A. A. Saunders
* Patrick J. Saunders
Richard L. Saunders
* William A. Saurman
Alice T. Saville
Florence M. Sawyer
Salvatore Sbrizza
* Mary Schneider
Louise C. Schoppelry
John F. Schottmiller
Marie E. Schulz
T. Herman Schulz
Gertrude M. Schwalb
Helen R. Scott
Edward C. Seaman
Mary F. Severino
Mary E. Sexton
Sarah M. Sharkey
* John S. Shaw
Francis J. Shea
Hilda S. Shead
Miriam H. Shead
Marion K. Sheedy
John J. Sheehan
Mary E. Sheehan
* Terrance F. Sheehan
Thomas L. Sheehan
* Anna G. Sheridan
Max Shurin
* Robert H. Siggins
Jennie Simmons
Walter E. Simmons
Hallie J. Simonson
* David W. Simpson
* Edith Sliney
Emma Sliney
Ernest E. Slocomb
William P. Slyne
Helen G. Smith

* R. H. Smith
* W. A. Smith
* W. A. Smith
* John A. Snowdon
Emma M. Snyder
* Augustus Sodergren
Jose D. Sousa
* R. A. Southworth
Beatrice E. Sparkes
Nellie C. Spillane
Mary G. Stack
Mary A. Stanton
Ida F. Stapleton
* Frederick P. Stearns
* Clara A. Steffens
Nicholas Stellatty
Margaret Marie Stewart
Nellie A. Stewart
* Robert C. Stoddard
Walter M. Stone
Benjamin Stoney
Henry H. Stoney
Julia M. Stout
Florence V. Strathdee
Marjorie M. Stynes
Annie Sullivan
Annie M. Sullivan
Catherine Sullivan
Delia A. Sullivan
* Elizabeth G. Sullivan
Frances B. Sullivan
Helen F. Sullivan
Helen V. Sullivan
* J. H. Sullivan
Louise P. Sullivan
Margaret L. Sullivan
* Mary Sullivan
Mary A. Sullivan
Mary E. Sullivan
Patrick J. Sullivan
Waldo F. Sutcliffe
Laura M. Sutter
* Katherine E. Sweeney
William L. Sweeney
Alice M. Swim
Nina L. Tame
Louise Tappan
* George Tate

B. E. Taylor
Caroline Taylor
Katherine R. Taylor
* Arthur Thomas
Gertrude Thomas
Helen M. Thomas
Cameron S. Thompson
* Charles E. Thurston
* Mary L. Timmins
George Tobin
* Hannah Toohey
Margaret E. Toomey
Harold E. Torngren
* Harry F. Torrey
Sarah A. Towle
* L. M. Tozier
Mary A. Tracey
* C. M. Travis
Jane Tregurtha
Anna A. Trevor
* Robert J. Trimble
* W. S. Tufts
Mary J. Tully
Josephine H. Turner
Minnie A. Turner
Bessie S. Tweed
* Thomas J. Urquhart
Harry C. Vail
Anthony R. Valenti
John B. Valentino
Jeanette Van Rees
* Thomas Viall
Rose C. Waggett
William Wallace
* F. E. Wallis
* Carrie Walsh
* John W. Walsh
Katherine H. Walsh
Margaret T. Walsh
Nellie Walsh
* F. W. Walthers
* Catherine L. Ward
Robert A. Wark
* Annie Warren

* George H. Watson
Ruth M. Webb
* Eugene Weibel
Agnes T. Welch
Annie L. Welch
Katherine A. Welch
Mary E. Welch
* Mary Welsh
Mary R. Wenners
Gertrude L. West
Marjorie E. West
Frank B. Wetherbee
Holden Whitaker
Anna White
* B. S. White
Beatrice A. White
Laura M. White
* Margaret F. White
Etta F. Whitney
Mary G. Whitstead
* William Wiles
* W. W. Willey
Bernard Williams
* W. D. Williams
Marjorie S. Wilmot
* Alexander Wilson
Anna L. Wilson
Ellen V. Wilson
* George Wilson
Phoebe A. Wilson
* Thomas H. Wilson
* Warren Wilson
* George H. Wood
* Emma F. Woodman
Frederick T. Wort
* Arthur H. Wright
Henry P. Wright
Henry S. Wright
Mary E. Wright
* M. Wrigley
* Elsie M. Yeo
Edith York
* B. H. Young

* Deceased

# OUR CENTENNIAL ASSOCIATES

I record herewith the names of many good friends of ours whose products or services and whose splendid cooperation have materially assisted us in reaching this, our Centennial Year.

A. & L. Sportswear Inc.
Abbott Co.
Abby-Kent Co.
Adams Brothers
Adams, Cushing & Foster, Inc.
Addressograph-Multigraph Corp.
Advance Pattern Co.
Alice Undergarment Co.
All State Garment Corp.
The All-Styles Hanger Co., Inc.
Allen Stationery Co., Inc.
Allied Appliance Co.
Allied Container Corp.
Allied Graphic Arts
Alps Sportswear Mfg. Co., Inc.
American Airlines
American Girl Shoe Co.
American Maid Co., Inc.
American Tourister Luggage
American Woolen Co., Inc.
The Amoline Mfg. Co.
Anthracite Overall Mfg. Co. Inc.
Archer Mills, Inc.
Elizabeth Arden Sales Corp.
The Asher Co.
Morris Asinof & Sons, Inc.
Atlantic Excelsior Co., Inc.

Attaya Co., Inc.
Avazis Bros. & Co.
Bacmo Postman Corp.
Bailey, Green & Elger, Inc.
Bali Brassiere Co., Inc.
Bancroft-Rellim Corp.
Baron-Abramson, Inc.
Barron-Anderson Company
A. Barsa & Bro., Inc.
Geo. G. Bashian
G. H. Bass & Co.
Albert Basse Associates
Bates Fabrics, Inc.
Beacon Frocks, Inc.
M. Beckerman & Sons, Inc.
Bellmore Dress Co., Inc.
Benmont Papers Inc.
Berkliff Undergarment Corp.
The Berkline Corp.
Berkshire Frocks Inc.
Bernard Sportswear, Inc.
Berry Clothing Co., Inc.
Biflex Foundations, Inc.
Bigelow-Sanford Carpet Co., Inc.
Bill & Caldwell, Inc.
Charles P. Blouin, Inc.
Blue Bell, Inc.

B. Blumenthal & Co., Inc.
Boit, Dalton & Church
Bonnie Bridal Fashions, Inc.
Milton Bradley Co.
Breslauer-Underberg, Inc.
Sue Brett, Inc.
W. F. Breuss
Robert Bruce Knitwear Co.
Buerkel & Co., Inc.
Bunny Bear Products
The Butterick Company, Inc.
Calpa Products Co.
Cardinal Cottons Corp.
Careful Cleaning Co.
Carlin & Fried, Inc.
Carry-Pack Co., Ltd.
Carter Rice and Company Corp.
William Carter Company
Castle Films
Catalina, Inc.
Cavanaugh & Earley, Inc.
Celex Products Corp.
Century Mailing, Inc.
Century Ribbon Mills, Inc.
Certified Fabrics Co.
Chadbourn Hosiery Mills, Inc.
Champion Bedding Co.
Charles & Co.
The L. J. Charrot Co., Inc.
Checker Taxi Co.
Chicago Curtain Stretcher Co.
The Christian Science Publishing
 Society
Cinderella Hat Co.
Cisco, Inc.
M. B. Claff & Sons, Inc.
Classy Leather Goods Corp.
Clayton Mfg. Co.
Clock Reel Yarns
Cohama Fabrics
Cohan Roth & Stiffson
Cohen Bros. Dress Corp.
College-Town Sportswear
Colman Levin Co.
Colonial Togs
Columbia-Ideal Quilting Co., Inc.
Comfort Pillow & Feather Co.
Comfy Manufacturing Co.

Commonwealth Clothing Company
Concord Woodworking Co., Inc.
Congress Sportswear Co.
John W. Conquest
Constantine Dress
Corham Artificial Flower Co.
Coro, Inc.
Court Square Press, Inc.
Craddock Furniture Corporation
Craddock-Terry Shoe Corp.
The Crown Corset Co.
B. T. Crump Co., Inc.
Cupid Foundations Inc.
Samuel Cupples Envelope Co., Inc.
Currick & Leiken Co., Inc.
Davenshire, Inc.
The Davidson Brothers Corp.
Davis Sportswear Co., Inc.
Debutogs Inc.
Decatur Garment Co.
Decatur & Hopkins Co.
Ralph A. DeConto Co.
Decorative Cabinet Corporation
Decorative Plant Corp.
Deltox Rug Co.
DeLuxe Parlor Furniture Co., Inc.
Dennison Mfg. Co.
George Dietz Company
Doeskin Products, Inc.
Jack Dominick Co.
John Donnelly & Sons
Downes Lumber Co.
Duofold, Inc.
Dutchess Underwear Corporation
Andrew Dutton Co.
Eagle Electric Supply Co., Inc.
The Eastern Company
Eastern Displays, Inc.
Eastern Ribbon Co.
Easy Washing Machine Corp.
Eaton Paper Corporation
Eby Shoe Corp.
Economy Wallpaper Company of
 Massachusetts
A. Elgart & Sons, Inc.
Ely & Walker
Emerson Radio of New England
Empire Carpet Corp.

111

Empire Curtain Mfg. Co.
Boston Envelope Co.
Equitable Paper Bag Co., Inc.
Bob Evans Uniform Company
L. B. Evans' Son Co.
Everlast Metal Products Corp.
Exeter Hosiery Mills, Inc.
M. Factor Co., Inc.
Fairclough & Gold, Inc.
Fashion Foundations Corp.
Fashion Park, Inc.
The Warren Featherbone Co.
Feine Trimming Co., Inc.
Felt & Tarrant Mfg. Co.
Finestone-Hahn Co.
David Fingerhut, Inc.
Jacob Finkelstein & Sons
Herman A. Finney, Inc.
Fisher Mannequin Repair Service
Fitwel Dress Co., Inc.
Fitzgibbons Co.
Flo-Jay Frocks, Inc.
Flower Modes, Ltd.
Forbes Lithograph Mfg. Co.
Formaid Co.
Forman & Gumner Co., Inc.
Formcraft, Inc.
Forsum Flower Co., Inc.
F. A. Foster & Co., Inc.
Frances Formals
Freedman-Roedelheim Co.
Freeman Mfg. Co.
H. Freeman & Son, Inc.
Friden Calculating Machine Agency
Gerald M. Friend Inc.
Frigidaire Sales Corp.
S. D. Frohlich Co.
Fuld Bros.
Fuldheim, Inc.
The Fuller Shirt Co., Inc.
G. & L. Mfg. Co.
Robert Gair Co., Inc.
Garay & Co., Inc.
Gardiner Shoe Co., Inc.
Prince Gardner
Gaylene's, Inc.
Charles S. Gelles & Son
Gem Crib and Cradle Co.

General Alarm Corporation
General Electric Appliances, Inc.
General Motors Corporation
Gibbs Oil Company
The Gibson Art Company
The A. C. Gilbert Company
Ginsburg Brothers, Inc.
Gladding, McBean & Co.
Glasgo Limited, Inc.
Glendale Knitting Corp.
Glensder Textile Corp.
Glenwood Range Co.
Glix-Brand Co., Inc.
Boston Globe
Globe Knitting Works
Gold-Sachs Co., Inc.
Gold Seal Rubber Co.
Goldin-Feldman Co.
Louis Goldsmith, Inc.
Ben Goodman & Son, Inc.
The Graham Corporation
Gralnick Brothers, Inc.
Grayblock Ribbon Co.
Daniel Green Co.
Greenspan & Co., Inc.
Gregg Mfg. Co.
Greneker Corp.
Grinnell Company, Inc.
Grossman Cap Co.
Grossman & Weissman, Inc.
Joseph Guttman & Bros.
The Haeger Potteries, Inc.
E. L. Ham Co.
Hampden Parlor Furniture Co., Inc.
Hampden Specialty Products, Inc.
Handmacher-Vogel, Inc.
Harper Method
Harris Raincoat Co. Inc.
Harwill Blouse Co., Inc.
Hayward Hosiery Company
H. C. H. Pant Co.
John Heathcoat & Co., Inc.
Hedstrom Union Co.
Heirloom Needlework Guild, Inc.
A. H. Heisey & Co.
The Heller Leather Co.
L. P. Henryson & Co., Inc.

Boston Herald-Traveler
  Corporation
J. F. Herne Co.
Hewes & Potter, Inc.
Heywood-Wakefield Company
Hickey-Freeman Co.
Hickok
M. M. Hirshberg Co.
Hirshon-Garfield, Inc.
Hoag & Provandie, Inc.
The Hoover Co.
Hough Shade Corp.
The House of Byer, Inc.
The Housh Co., Inc.
A. T. Howard Company
The Howell Co.
Hudnut Sales Co., Inc.
Hudson Hosiery Co.
Ideal Novelty and Toy Company
Imperial Glass Corp.
Ingber, Inc.
International Dry Goods Co., Inc.
International Harvester Co.
International Shoe Co.
Interwoven Stocking Co.
Jayhawk Mfg. Co., Inc.
Jerry Coat Co., Inc.
The Jewish Advocate
Joelle Coats, Inc.
Johnson Brothers
Johnson-Stephens & Shinkle Shoe Co.
Jones, McDuffee & Stratton Corp.
Joslin Showcase & Fixture Co.
Joyce, Inc.
Kaplan & Elias, Inc.
The Kaynee Company
Kayson Sportwear Corp.
Thomas F. Kearns Electrical Supply
  Co.
Keith, Keith & McCain, Inc.
Kemp & Beatley, Inc.
Ken Products, Inc.
Kendall Mills
Kernettes, Inc.
Helen Kingsley, Inc.
G. Klein & Son
I. B. Kleinert Rubber Co.
The Kling Factories

Knickerbocker Toy Co.
Knit Products Sales Co.
Kops Brothers, Inc.
A. Kreamer, Inc.
Kurtzman Bros.
Landmark Dress Co., Inc.
F. J. Lawson Electric Co.
Leacock & Company, Inc.
LeMonde Corset Company
LeRoi Hosiery Co., Inc.
The Levenson Co.
Henry Levine Co., Inc.
Victor Levine
Isidore Levitt
M. S. Levy & Sons, Inc.
Liberty Laboratories Corp.
Sam Lichtenberg, Inc.
Harry Lichtman
The Literary Guild of America Inc.
Loman Electric Supply Co., Inc.
Thomas Long Co.
Lowenthal Trimming Corp.
Joseph Love, Inc.
Lovell & Covel Co.
Lubin-Weeker Co., Inc.
Mabs Inc.
MacGregor Goldsmith, Inc.
MacTaggart Sportswear, Inc.
Maddox Table Co.
Jim Mahoney Sho-Cards
Maiden Form Brassiere Co., Inc.
Majestic Specialties Inc.
Malino Veilings
Mallory Hats
Fred Maloof Co., Inc.
Manchester Knitted Fashions, Inc.
Marketing Associates
Marshall, Meadows & Stewart, Inc.
Mason & Snow, Inc.
Massachusetts Mattress Co.
Master Motion Picture Co.
Mavest, Inc.
Mayflower Products, Inc.
B. McCabe & Sons
The McDonald Company
L. H. McIsaac Co.
William N. McKenna Co.
McLoughlin Mfg. Co.

I. Medoff Company
Mendel-Drucker, Inc.
The Mengel Company
Merchandise Clearing Co.
The Mersman Bros. Corp.
Messmore & Damon, Inc.
Metric Hosiery Co., Inc.
A. I. Meyer Corp.
Milhender Distributors, Inc.
Miller Paper Co.
Minkplastic Corp.
Minute Mop Co.
Wm. H. Mitchell & Son Co.
Mittelman, Bernstein & Co.
M. K. M. Knitting Mills, Inc
Modern Mfg. Co., Inc.
Mojud Hosiery Co., Inc.
Monroe Moore Co.
Moore Business Forms, Inc.
Morgantown Glassware Guild Inc.
Moriarty Van Lines
Morse's, Inc.
Motor Car Company of New England
The Mueck-Cary Co., Inc.
F. A. Mulcahy & Sons
Mutual Brief Case Co., Inc.
Najeeb, Inc.
National Associated Mills, Inc.
The National Cash Register Co.
National Sewing Machine Co.
National Transitads Inc.
Nawi, Noonoo & Co., Inc.
D. H. Neumann Co., Inc.
New England Bedding Co.
New England Confectionery Co.
New England Decorator's Supply Co.
New England Electric Service Co.
New England Mackintosh Co., Inc.
New England Millinery, Inc.
The New England Robe Corp.
I. Newman & Sons, Inc.
Boston News Clip
Nichols & Stone Co.
K. Nissan, Inc.
Norcross, Inc.
Northeastern Distributors, Inc.
North Star Woolen Mill Co.

S. W. Nu Enamel Co., Inc.
Nylo-Knit Sportswear, Inc.
Joseph M. O'Callaghan Co.
O. K. Trouser Mfg. Co.
Murray Oliphant
Onondaga Silk Co., Inc.
J. I. Originals Inc.
Guy Ormandy Orchestras
Owens-Illinois Glass Co. Inc.
Palm Beach Company
Pandora Knitwear, Inc.
Paradise Shoes
Par-Form Foundations, Inc.
Pam Paterson, Inc.
Peacock Shoes
Pearl Preview Shoe Co.
L. I. Pendleton & Sons
Pequot Mills
Periodical Publishers' Service Bureau, Inc.
Personal Products Corporation
Philadelphia Carpet Co.
Philharmonic Radio Corporation
Pickwick Knitting Mills, Inc.
Plymouth Novelty Co.
Poirette Corsets, Inc.
Polan, Katz & Co., Inc.
Chas. Porder Mfg. Co.
Porter Construction Co.
Boston Post
John E. Postley, Inc.
The John Robert Powers Products Co., Inc.
Leo Prager, Inc.
S. D. Prince Co.
Princess Charming
Princess Peggy, Inc.
Prival & Peyser, Inc.
Protex Products Co., Inc.
Wm. F. Prout & Sons
Puritan Mills, Inc.
Quality Paper Box Co.
Queen Valley Fabrics, Inc.
R. & H. Pant Co.
Rand Avery-Gordon Taylor, Inc.
G. H. Rauschenberg Co.
The Raycurt Co.
Boston Record-American

Recordak Corporation
Reefer-Galler, Inc.
Regent Ltd.
Reinhardt Mfg. Co.
Reinis Coat & Suit Co., Inc.
Reliance Mfg. Co.
Rennie Mfg. Co., Inc.
Rest-Well Products, Inc.
Revilo, Inc.
Revlon Products Corp.
Rhea Mfg. Co.
Rice-Stix, Inc.
Richelieu Pearls
N. J. Richman Co.
Riegel & Dechter, Inc.
The Rite Form Corset Co., Inc.
Rockland Sportswear, Inc.
Rose Brothers, Inc.
Rose-Derry Company
Rose Shower Curtain Mfg. Co. Inc.
Ross & Oberleder Fabrics Corp.
Royal Curtain Mfg. Co.
Royal Robes
Royal Typewriter Co., Inc.
Rubinstein & Haibloom, Inc.
Helena Rubinstein
Rust Craft Publishers
Salem Brothers
Salmanson & Co., Inc.
Salta Knitting Mills, Inc.
Sampson-Katzenberg
L. J. Samuels & Co., Inc.
Sandler of Boston
Schack's, Inc.
I. Schneierson & Sons, Inc.
M. C. Schrank Co.
David E. Schwab & Co., Inc.
Schwartz & Rosenfeld
The Selby Shoe Co.
Semca Watch Corporation
Sharon Robe Co., Inc.
Shaw Furniture Co., Inc.
Shaw Publications, Inc.
Shelburne Shirt Co., Inc.
The Sherwin-Williams Co.
Shipman & Baker
Sho-Card Printing
Shulton, Inc.

Jacob Siegel Co.
Silin Mfg. Co.
Silk-O-Lite Mfg. Corp.
Silvestri Art Mfg. Co.
The Simone Co., Inc.
Alexander Smith & Sons Carpet Co.
Leon Snow Co.
Southern Furniture Co.
A. G. Spalding & Bros., Inc.
Sparks, Inc.
Sportleigh
The Boston Sport-Light
Sport-Modes of Boston
Standard Knitting Mills, Inc.
Stanley & Stanley, Inc.
Stardust, Inc.
State Upholstering Co., Inc.
Harry G. Stauf
A. Stein & Company
Stern, Merritt Co., Inc.
John B. Stetson Company
The Stetson Shoe Co., Inc.
Stone's Express, Inc.
Store Service Press, Inc.
The Strouse, Adler Co.
The Strouse-Baer Co.
Studios of Waltham
Stylerite Mfg. Co.
Sugarman Brothers, Inc.
The Superb Glove Co.
Superior Knitting Co.
Superior Petticoat Co., Inc.
Symphonic Radio and Electronic
   Corp.
Syracuse Ladies Handbags
The Tappan Stove Co.
The Taylor-Bramley Co., Inc.
W. H. W. Teele Co.
Tennessee Tufting Co.
Textron Inc.
Tiffin Glassmasters
Timely Accessories, Inc.
George A. Tirone Studio
Tobe and Associates, Inc.
Topakian & Co., Inc.
Town and Cottage Frocks
Transit Advertisers, Inc.
Trifari, Krussman and Fishel, Inc.

Tuch Dress Corp.
Albert Turner
Underwood Corporation
Union Carbide & Carbon Corp.
Union Underwear Co., Inc.
U. S. Bedford Textile Co.
United States Rubber Co.
United States Trunk Co., Inc.
Van Raalte
Vanity Fair Mills, Inc.
Vanity Sports Wear
Vatco Mfg. Co., Inc.
The Verplex Co.
Victory Belt Co. Inc.
Villa-Zigmund & Co. Inc.
Walker Stetson Co.
Warshauer & Franck, Inc.
Weber Originals, Inc.
The Weiman Co.
Weinberg-Weinberg-Alpern

W. W. Welch, Inc.
Wembly, Inc.
West End & Hub Spring Co., Inc.
WHDH, Boston
The White Motor Company
White Swan Uniforms, Inc.
Frank M. Whiting & Co.
Whitney Bros., Inc.
M. J. Whittall Associates, Inc.
D. G. Williams, Inc.
Wolfson & Greenbaum, Inc.
Woodmere Hats Inc.
The Wooster Rubber Co.
Allen B. Wrisley Co.
The Yankee Network, Inc.
    WNAC-TV, WNAC-AM-FM
York Street Flax Spinning Co., Inc.
Jack Young Company
Youth Guild, Inc.